A STATEMENT OF
BASIC
ACCOUNTING THEORY

American Accounting Association

i

LIBRARY OF CONGRESS CATALOG NUMBER 66-26930

PRINTED IN THE UNITED STATES OF AMERICA

American Accounting Association

COMMITTEE TO PREPARE A STATEMENT

OF

BASIC ACCOUNTING THEORY

Norton M. Bedford	Russell H. Morrison
R. Lee Brummet	Roland F. Salmonson
Neil C. Churchill	George H. Sorter
Paul E. Fertig	Lawrence L. Vance

Charles T. Zlatkovich, *Chairman*

CONTENTS

PREFACE

The American Accounting Association has a consistent record of activity in the development of accounting principles, standards, and accounting theory generally. From 1936 through 1964, committees of the Association published, under a variety of titles, four complete statements and a total of thirteen of a supplementary nature, eight of which related to the 1948 Statement and five to the 1957 Revision. The first complete statement, published in 1936 by the Executive Committee of the Association, is a landmark both in the work of the Association and in the development of accounting theory. Although comparable effort was invested in subsequent statements, it is unlikely that any of them received equivalent attention or constituted an equivalent contribution.

Believing that the "series" inaugurated with the 1936 statement had served its purpose and that the time had come for the Association to undertake a new and different kind of effort, the 1964 Executive Committee authorized appointment of a committee with the following broad charge:

> The charge of this committee is to develop an integrated statement of basic accounting theory which will serve as a guide to educators, practitioners, and others interested in accounting. The statement should include adequate support for any position taken and sufficient explanation to provide clarity, yet be as concise as feasible.
>
> The committee should not feel bound in any way by the format or content of previous statements issued by this or other organizations.
>
> Among the subjects the committee may want to consider are the role, nature, and limitations of accounting, both now and in the future; the appropriate conceptual framework for a coordinated statement of accounting theory; and the possibility of implementing its conclusions.
>
> This charge is given with a reminder of the unique opportunity available to the American Accounting Association to contribute to the advancement of accountancy through the conduct of fundamental research and the dissemination of the results of such research.

Members of the committee accepted appointment with enthusiasm and have pressed toward conclusion of their assignment vigorously, unselfishly devoting much time and energy to the production of a statement which marks a new type of accomplishment for the Association. Some will applaud its recommendations; others will criticize; most will find it controversial in some part. We join the committee, which has served throughout our terms, in offering it to you as another in the Association's continuing attempts to advance the discipline of accounting. The members of the committee deserve full credit for the extent of their effort and the quality of this statement.

ROBERT K. MAUTZ
President, 1965

HERBERT E. MILLER
President, 1965-1966

The Committee to Prepare a Statement of Basic Accounting Theory first met in October 1964, the month it was appointed. We were urged to complete our project before August, 1966 (Fiftieth Anniversary Meeting), if possible. The Committee worked diligently toward that goal and met 8 times for a total of 20 days, usually with 100% attendance There were also several subcommittee meetings.

In retrospect, it seems to me taking longer would likely have resulted in an expression of essentially the same ideas with different and perhaps fewer words. Consensus on the basic content was reached fairly early; thereafter, words changed, but fundamental ideas were largely unaffected. One reason for this brief recital of the Committee's history is to note the fact that during this same period other investigators working independently came up with some of the same ideas.

CHARLES T. ZLATKOVICH, Chairman,
Committee to Prepare a Statement of
Basic Accounting Theory.

CHAPTER I

INTRODUCTION

The charge of this committee was to prepare a statement of basic accounting theory. We define "theory" as a cohesive set of hypothetical, conceptual, and pragmatic principles forming a general frame of reference for a field of study. In developing this statement, the committee has sought:

(1) to identify the field of accounting so that useful generalizations about it can be made and a theory developed;

(2) to establish standards by which accounting information may be judged;

(3) to point out possible improvements in accounting practice;

(4) to present a useful framework for accounting researchers seeking to extend the uses of accounting and the scope of accounting subject matter as needs of society expand.

The committee has not attempted to consider all the individual accounting practices that might be the subject of recommendations in the light of standards formulated in this statement. Certain general recommendations for the modification of accounting practice are made and a few important specific problem areas are also the subject of recommendations (Chapter III and Appendices A and B). However, the major effort of the committee has been to establish a foundation of concepts from which particular practices can be judged.

The committee defines accounting as the process of identifying, measuring, and communicating economic information to permit informed judgments and decisions by users of the information. The concept of economics referred to in the preceding sentence holds that economics is concerned with any situation in which a choice must be made involving scarce resources. The term "measurement" includes the choice of an accounting method, as last-in, first-out to measure inventory or deferral of federal income taxes to measure income.

This definition of accounting is broader than that expressed in other statements of accounting theory. There is no implication that accounting information is necessarily based only on transaction data, and it will be shown that information based on various types of non-transaction data meet the standards for accounting information. Although

1

measurements of assets and periodic earnings qualify as accounting information, our definition of accounting is not limited to these measurements, nor is the concept limited to those entities in which earning periodic profits is a primary objective.

This committee has focused its attention on the entire area of accounting (as defined above) as its field of inquiry, for the purpose of presenting a statement that it believes will prove useful as a frame of reference and as a guide to accountants in carrying out the accounting function. In so doing, the committee has conceived of theory as a coherent set of concepts explaining and guiding the accountant's action in identifying, measuring, and communicating economic information.

The committee's statement envisages application of the accounting process not only to business operated for profit, but also to the activities of individuals, fiduciaries, governmental units, charitable enterprises, and similar entities. Information systems are designed to serve managers and others in carrying out the organizational objectives of entities in which profitability is not the sole or even an important objective as well, of course, as in business entities. Economic considerations, broadly conceived, are of major importance in planning action and controlling operations to achieve the planned objectives for all entities. While this statement may, because of certain illustrations, appear to be directed primarily toward profit-making enterprises, virtually all of the observations and recommendations are applicable with equal force to organizations with other objectives.

This statement covers communication of economic information to internal management as well as to external users; its generalizations concerning the identification, measurement, and communication process are intended to apply regardless of the identity of the user of the information. Standards for accounting information are developed that can be applied to almost any question of accounting propriety.

In the past, accounting for external use has been based upon concepts of income and wealth. Accounting for internal managerial use, on the other hand, while based broadly upon economic concepts, must also include the concepts arising from the growing body of knowledge about management. This is particularly true of the parts of this knowledge and technology which are now sufficiently objective, well documented, and extensive to be regarded as essentially a theory of management. The committee believes that as this theory continues to develop, external reporting will be expanded to encompass more measurements of managerial actions, structure, and perhaps even plans. For the near future, however, it is expected that management theory will have much more influence on internal than upon external accounting reports. For this reason, the statement treats external and internal reporting in separate chapters.

Approach to the Subject

The committee's approach to the formulation of this statement of accounting theory includes the following steps:

1. The general need for accounting information on the part of users and potential users is indicated in the definition of accounting as primarily a need for information useful in economizing, when the latter term is understood to refer to the use of all kinds of limited resources. Major categories of this activity are set out later and discussed in this chapter under the heading of "The Objectives of Accounting."

2. Standards for accounting information and guidelines for communicating accounting information are presented and defined in Chapter II. In establishing these standards, the all-inclusive criterion is the usefulness of the information. But simply to say that accounting information must be useful is too general a statement to be helpful in formulating a theory. Usefulness is necessarily determined through the eyes of the user; and especially in the case of accounting information, users often are not competent to determine what information is most useful to them or at least are not articulate in stating their needs. Fortunately it is possible to divide the criterion of usefulness into standards which are more susceptible to measurement and implementation. These criteria (standards for accounting information) have been formulated by asking, "What characteristics should accounting information have in order to be useful?" If the standards selected are established as necessary and sufficient to basic accounting theory, they will serve not only as yardsticks against which current practice can be judged and recommendations for improvement made, but will also assist in establishing the scope of accounting. Not only should information that meets the standards be included in accounting; all information that does not meet the standards should be excluded. We recognize, in this connection, that different uses of information imply that various degrees of conformance with the standards may be appropriate for different cases, and that the application of any standard requires judgment on the part of persons qualified to exercise it.

3. The use of the standards is illustrated by showing how they should be applied in general purpose financial reports for external users (Chapter III) and in reporting for internal management (Chapter IV). Current accounting practice is judged in the light of the standards, and suggestions for improvement are made.

4. Enlarging of the area of accounting is suggested by extending the assumptions regarding the objectives, scope, and methods of current accounting practice and by applying the standards to areas presently considered to be outside the purview of accounting, but which are includible within the scope of measurement and communication of economic data (Chapter V).

The Objectives of Accounting

The objectives of accounting are to provide information for the following purposes:

1. Making decisions concerning the use of limited resources, including the identification of crucial decision areas, and determination of objectives and goals.

2. Effectively directing and controlling an organization's human and material resources.

3. Maintaining and reporting on the custodianship of resources.

4. Facilitating social functions and controls.

Decisions involving limited resources are made by individuals acting in their own behalf, such as the stockholders or creditors of a firm, by agents serving in fiduciary capacities, or by individuals or groups in business firms, in government, in not-for-profit organizations and elsewhere. Success in decision making must be judged in terms of the goals of those in whose behalf the decisions are made, subject to legal and moral constraints imposed by society. The information appropriate to a specific decision can be determined only after the objectives have been specified; but it frequently happens that objectives are not clearly perceived or may be in conflict. Those who make decisions do not always recognize the complexities of the information appropriate to their decisions. Where the underlying conditions necessarily require that complex information be reported and where goals of interested parties are in conflict, the experience and skills of the accountant are essential if the standards set out in Chapter II are to be met.

In the area of internal management—administrative direction and control—accounting information is used to facilitate the formulation and execution of plans. Through systematic record-keeping, special investigations, and analyses of data, accounting makes possible efficiency in the acquisition, maintenance and use of the resources required by the plans. Accounting also plays a role in the motivation of individuals and groups charged with developing and carrying out plans, and it provides the major means of appraising the effectiveness with which individuals and groups perform their assignments.

The function of stewardship or custodianship may be a managerial function, as in the cases of boards of directors of enterprises organized for profit, or it may be a fiduciary function, as in the cases of trusteeships and guardianships. The interests of society are paramount in defining this function and have been expressed in the corporation codes of the various states and in the laws governing the activities and responsibilities of fiduciaries. Providing information relating to compliance with these laws is essentially an accounting function.

Other social functions in which accounting plays important roles include taxation, the prevention of fraud in a variety of contexts, governmental regulation of utilities, the activities of government in the general regulation and stimulation of commerce, management-labor relations, and the preparation of statistics on economic activity for the use of all interested persons. The accounting objective in this area is to facilitate the operations of organized society for the welfare of all.

The Scope of Accounting

Accounting contributes information regarding activities which form a continuous stream on which many distinct points may be identified. In the main, they are economic activities. The associated informational needs include references to historical transactions, as in the traditional accounting statements, and to future plans and expectations, as in budgets, standard costs, and the like. Although accounting has often been thought of as essentially historical in nature, it is important to recognize that emphasis upon those accounting techniques that deal with future plans and expectations has been increasing, and that this trend may be expected to continue. Furthermore, the historical record is kept, as all history is studied, for its lessons to be used as a guide to the future. This is another way of saying that the informational demands upon accounting are the requirements of the decisions in which it is used, and that these almost always have an orientation to the future. Accounting is a measurement and communication process which may be applied to a variety of subjects. Most applications of accounting have dealt with economic resources (traditionally defined) and the bulk of the present discussion is oriented to these applications. Nevertheless, as suggested more fully in Chapter V, accounting need not be confined to such subject matter.

The Methods of Accounting

Accounting methodology includes the various techniques and procedures used by accountants in measuring, describing, and interpreting economic data to users. These techniques include generally accepted accounting principles and practices, as well as alternatives which may not meet the criterion of "general acceptance" but for which there is substantial authoritative support. Their application results in abstract expression of the activities of acquiring, using, and disposing of economic resources. Specified attributes of economic resources are described by specified methods for measuring the magnitude of the attributes in dollars or some other unit. The results of this descriptive and interpretive process are expressed in the form of accounting reports.

The purpose in developing a theory of accounting is to establish standards for judging the acceptability of accounting methods. Procedures that meet the standards should be employed in the practice of accounting; those failing to meet the standards should be rejected. The absence of an accepted theory of accounting has led many accountants to equate "accounting theory" with the sum total of all accounting practices currently in use. They thus lack logical criteria for accepting or rejecting various practices.

In this statement of basic accounting theory, the committee has formulated standards that will provide means of *accepting or rejecting accounting methods* currently in use, or methods proposed for future use. For instance, as various methods for measuring the current cost of plant and equipment assets are proposed, it should be possible to determine whether a particular method should or should not be accepted as an addition to accounting practice. Applying the standards has led the committee to the conclusion that important changes in accounting practice should be made.

CHAPTER II

ACCOUNTING STANDARDS

Four basic standards are recommended as providing criteria to be used in evaluating potential accounting information: relevance, verifiability, freedom from bias, and quantifiability. Adherence to some or all of these standards may be partial. As with all standards, exercise of judgment as to the adequacy with which they are met is essential.

Relevance is the primary standard and requires that the information must bear upon or be usefully associated with actions it is designed to facilitate or results desired to be produced. Known or assumed informational needs of potential users are of paramount importance in applying this standard.

Verifiability requires that essentially similar measures or conclusions would be reached if two or more qualified persons examined the same data. It is important because accounting information is commonly used by persons who have limited access to the data. The less the proximity to the data, the greater the desirable degree of verifiability becomes. Verifiability is also important because users of accounting information sometimes have opposing interests.

Freedom from bias means that facts have been impartially determined and reported. It also means that techniques used in developing data should be free of built-in bias. Biased information may be quite useful and tolerable internally but it is rarely acceptable for external reporting.

Quantifiability relates to the assignment of numbers to the information being reported. Money is the most common but not the only quantitative measure used by accountants. When accountants present non-quantitative information in compliance with the other standards they should not imply its measurability. Conversely, when quantitative information is reported without a caveat the accountant must assume responsibility for its measurability.

Five guidelines for communication of accounting information are recommended. They are:

1. Appropriateness to expected use.
2. Disclosure of significant relationships.
3. Inclusion of environmental information.
4. Uniformity of practice within and among entities.
5. Consistency of practices through time.

We recognize that there is some overlap between the four standards and the five guidelines; the latter are important but less fundamental.

STANDARDS FOR ACCOUNTING INFORMATION

Accounting information must be useful to people acting in various capacities both inside and outside of the entity concerned. It must be useful in the formulation of objectives, the making of decisions, or the direction and control of resources to accomplish objectives. The utility of information lies in its abilitiy to reduce uncertainty about the actual state of affairs of concern to the user. The committee feels that adherence to the standards for accounting information, as proposed below, will result in a marked reduction of this uncertainty.

The committee recommends four basic standards for accounting information as follows:

1. Relevance.
2. Verifiability.
3. Freedom from bias.
4. Quantifiability.

These standards provide criteria to be used in evaluating potential accounting information. They constitute a basis for inclusion or exclusion of data as accounting information. If these criteria, taken as a whole, are not adequately met, the information is unacceptable. On the other hand, economic data which adequately fulfill these criteria represent accounting material that must be considered for reporting.

Adequate fulfillment of these criteria does not require complete adherence to any one or all of these standards under all circumstances. It is possible to realize them more fully in some cases than in others. Further, it is basic to recognize that different uses call for different degrees of adherence. The communication of information which reflects only marginal conformity to one or more of these standards requires disclosure of this characteristic to the users of the information. This marginal conformity may relate to particular figures, to an entire report, or to the system that produced the information.

Thus these standards serve two purposes: first, they constitute a basis or point of departure for appraising the validity or adequacy of any accounting method in view of the information that it produces; second, they provide a mechanism for determining the degree of compliance required for information related to a particular use.

It is important to understand thoroughly the essential nature of the four standards and to examine their use in establishing suitable degrees of conformance of potential accounting information. The nature of the standards as such is considered in the remainder of this section.

The Standard of Relevance

For information to meet the standard of relevance, it must bear upon or be usefully associated with the action it is designed to facilitate or the result it is desired to produce. This requires that either the information or the act of communicating it exert influence or have the potential for exerting influence on the designated actions. For this influence to be exerted, the information must be available in a form and at a time for it to be useful.

As there are differing degrees of usefulness, so are there different degrees of relevance for different purposes. For example, the original recorded cost of a building twenty years ago might have been $200,000 and similar buildings might cost $400,000 today. Each item of information has relevance for a particular use. The $200,000 figure has relevance in the calculation of depreciation for income tax purposes under an historical-cost-based income tax system. The $400,000 figure has virtually no relevance for this purpose. To the person considering what price to pay for the building, the $400,000 figure has a high degree of relevance and the $200,000 has virtually no relevance. The original owner of the building who is now contemplating its sale is interested in its sale price and the total financial consequences of such a sale transaction. To him, each item of information has relevance and both items together have greater relevance than either standing alone.

The accounting function should, under many circumstances, provide information with a high degree of relevance to a specific intended use although it may have little relevance to any other. When this is done, care must be taken to disclose the limitations of the information to prevent the possible assumption of universal relevance. To have information used for purposes for which it has no relevance is likely to be worse than having no information at all. Not only may decisions be influenced wrongly, but the user may be diverted from an effort to acquire relevant information.

The standard of relevance is primary among the four recommended standards. Although not sufficient as a sole criterion, it represents a necessary characteristic for all accounting information. None of the other standards has this position of primacy. Nevertheless, the committee believes that the process of judging accounting information should involve a combined and simultaneous consideration of all four standards. The required degree of adherence to each standard is conditioned by the degree to which the other standards are met. The relative significance of each standard depends upon the nature of the information and its intended use. Both the minimum conformity required with any one of the standards and rates of substitution (trade-off) among the four standards are conditioned by the circumstances.

The Standard of Verifiability

Verifiability is that attribute of information which allows qualified individuals working independently of one another to develop essentially similar measures or conclusions from an examination of the same evidence, data, or records. This standard does not always require identical results. It may, in some instances, allow variations within known limits. Verifiability needs to be based upon well-understood criteria governing recognition, classification, and valuation of the items under consideration and consistency in the application of the criteria. It is primarily concerned with the availability and adequacy of evidence attesting to the validity of the data being considered.

One of the basic characteristics of accounting is that it frequently serves parties who have opposing interests. It furnishes information to both buyers and sellers; to taxpayers and tax collectors; to debtors and to creditors. In these situations, the information is likely to be prepared by or on the behalf of one of the parties although it is used by both of the parties. It is essential that some means be available to assure users with varied interests that the information is dependable. This condition may be met by the use of established rules and conventions which, when applied consistently, leave a trail of evidence and procedures that can be verified. For example, the price at which a listed security was traded on a particular day ordinarily constitutes sufficient evidence to verify the security's value at that date, but the value of the same security three months hence is less verifiable for there is no present sufficient evidence of a price, apart from a valid offer to buy or contract to sell.

The standard of verifiability is a necessary attribute of accounting information in order to make possible a reliance by persons who have neither access to the underlying records nor competence to audit them. It is also necessary, in some degree, to make possible the presentation of an independent accountant's opinion. This reference to interpersonal and third party relationships should not obscure the fact that the verifiability standard is important to accounting information generally. Information prepared for internal use, or even personal use by the accountant involved, requires some degree of verifiability. Ignoring the standard in such cases involves the danger of confusing significant facts with personal or organizational bias. The same degree of verifiability may not be required for information used internally as that required for information used in external reports. For internal purposes, subjective estimates, especially forecasts, may be useful because of their high degree of relevance even though they possess a very low degree of verifiability.

The Standard of Freedom from Bias

It is possible for accounting information to possess high degrees of relevance and verifiability and yet be biased in favor of some parties and detrimental to others. This bias may result from use of inappropriate techniques or it may be of a personal nature. The use of plant-wide overhead rates may produce a statistical bias in product cost information. Information prepared by the accountant of a corporation selling its assets to another entity may be biased in the direction of high asset valuations for possible personal gain.

The standard of freedom from bias is advocated because of the many users accounting serves and the many uses to which it may be put. The presence of bias which may serve the needs of one set of users cannot be assumed to aid or even leave unharmed the interests of others. It is conceivable that biased information could properly be introduced if it would aid one group without injuring the position of any other, but this conclusion cannot be reached with certainty in external reporting, where all potential users must be considered. Thus, bias should be avoided in external general purpose reports. Information susceptible to bias may sometimes be useful in internal reporting, where all probable users may be determined, but in such cases the limitations of the data should be clearly disclosed. When other standards are met equally well and there is a choice between biased and unbiased information, the unbiased information is preferable.

The Standard of Quantifiability

Accounting in its historical aspect is primarily a device for expressing economic activity in terms of money. Yet such expressions are not the whole of either accounting or of quantification, for quantification can be considered as the association of a number with a transaction or an activity where the numbers assigned obey prescribed arithmetic laws or procedures. There is no specification as to whether these numbers represent dollars, feet, tons, or degrees Fahrenheit. In order to distinguish quantification in general from the assignment of dollar or other monetary measures, the latter may be considered as a special case of quantification and referred to as valuation. Thus, without restricting accounting to any rigidly pre-determined area of activity, it can be said that the primary, if not the total concern of accountants, is with quantification and quantified data. In fact, wherever the accountant is involved outside the area of quantification he should exert special care for he has a particular obligation derived from the historical association of his practice with quantified data. He should make sure there is no implication of measurability when non-quantitative information is presented and be certain that measurability is characteristic of such information as is presented in quantitative form without a caveat. This does not deny the possibility of improving the measurement process in accounting. Indeed, suggestions are made to that effect in the remainder of this section.

The quantification of data adds usefulness. Measurement in its most primitive aspect involves forming classes of equivalent objects or events. This is the basis of identifying, recognizing, and labeling ordinary objects. Moving up the scale of measurement, more information is communicated about the items measured. Progression is from statements of equality (within classes) through knowledge of greater than or less than (or positional relationships) to statements about the magnitude of differences, and finally to ratios. Thus, quantification conveys more information than strictly qualitative statements and conveys it in a way that provides for obtaining further knowledge through mathematical operations. Qualitative information is of course important, but the accounting function emphasizes meaningful quantification represented by numbers to increase usefulness.

The use of numbers raises some further issues. Some attribute or characteristic of an item or an activity under examination is quantified. Consideration must be given to the characteristic selected, the measure applied, and the manner in which this is accomplished. In accounting, the attribute most often selected is economic usefulness (in a narrowly defined sense) and the measure most often applied is dollars of value or cost.

There is no *prima facie* reason why a narrow economic significance should be the only attribute measured by accounting, although it is no doubt the most important. There is also no reason why the only measure applied should be "value" in terms of dollars. It is entirely conceivable that accounting should deal with various measures and do so in a systematic form, say, a vector or number of measures. Finally, there is no reason why a single number—a point value or deterministic measure—must always be used. The transaction or event dealt with might be represented by more than one number or dollar value. In this case, a range or interval estimate for the event can be used. Interval estimates can be dealt with in a rigorous manner by statistical techniques and can and should be included within the scope of the accountant's function. The development of accounting should keep pace with economics and managerial technology, and this requires a broader use of quantitative methods.

GUIDELINES FOR COMMUNICATING ACCOUNTING INFORMATION

The development of accounting information is only part of the accounting function. A necessary companion aspect of the function is the development of the communication process so that information can be transmitted and so that those to whom information is provided understand it and its potential usefulness.

The nature of the transmission problem may be visualized by recognizing the accountant as an observer of economic or related activities (past, present, or future) which he records in abstract form using descriptive words and numbers. If the accounting information is good and the accountant is properly skilled, these abstractions will present an accurate model or picture of the underlying activity. To convey an accurate picture of the activity to the user, the accountant must use abstractions, but his objective is always to convey an understanding of the activity rather than merely to transmit words and numbers.

The traditional approach to communication of accounting information requires a high degree of understanding of the measurement process on the part of the user. This process is complex and, when combined with the technical nature of the material, places a significant burden on the user. To ease this burden, uniformity of meaning of words and numbers used in accounting is essential. Beyond this, rules or guidelines for use of accounting abstractions are needed to assure that the underlying activity is revealed and not obscured or distorted by the reporting process.

Communication is a vital link in accounting activity. It is of no less importance than that of developing the information itself, yet the process is a link which must depend upon and follow the information development stage. Further, there is considerable overlap between the standards governing communication and the standards governing the nature of accounting information *per se*. Recognizing these characteristics, the committee has chosen to give a separate treatment to the area of communications to aid in clarity, but to refer to the basic communication requirements as "guidelines" rather than "standards."

Published financial reports may have an effect upon a very large unknown number of persons, including many who are not versed in accounting. The standards for accounting information given earlier in this chapter apply with special force to accounting reports designed for use by persons outside the firm. This is also true of the guidelines for communication. The guidelines that follow are couched in terms appropriate to current accounting problems. They are consistent with the basic essentials of communication theory. The committee proposes five guidelines for communication of accounting information:

1. Appropriateness to expected use.
2. Disclosure of significant relationships.
3. Inclusion of environmental information.
4. Uniformity of practices within and among entities.
5. Consistency of practices through time.

Appropriateness to Expected Use

This guideline requires that reports be prepared with the intended user's needs in mind. It implies a conveyance of information to the cognizant decision-maker that is both relevant and timely. It requires that reports rendered for different purposes clearly indicate the scope of their usefulness. This guideline has an obvious application to internal reports, where very special or even unique needs may be served. Its application to external reports requires that techniques adopted for some special purposes be excluded from reports destined for creditors or investors generally. There is no substantial problem in obtaining information necessary for such prominent special reports as income tax returns and reports to regulatory bodies since the authorities requiring them have the power to specify the form and accounting methods to be used. It would be helpful if public authorities would consider carrying out their mandates with accounting reports of more general usefulness.

The influence of any special information needs should be isolated from general reporting. An example of a practice contrary to this results from the requirement that last-in, first-out inventory methods are allowable for tax purposes only if they are regularly used by the taxpayer for record-keeping and reporting purposes; the effect of this is to force the method into a general use which it would probably not have attained if it were not linked to a tax saving. Insofar as they must be different, reports prepared for special users should not have any necessary effect upon general purpose reports. The economy often claimed as justification for using one measurement method for all purposes fortunately tends to become less important as electronic data processing advances. In general, it is expected that accounting will be able to comply more fully with the communication guideline of appropriateness to expected use in the future than in the past.

Disclosure of Significant Relationships

Reports should be prepared to permit observation of significant financial and operating activities of the firm. This reporting guideline requires that the information be so presented that the user may understand and evaluate the underlying activity generating the data. Reporting accumulated charges for depreciation and for doubtful accounts as deductions from plant and accounts receivable are examples of appropriate response to the need for disclosure of significant relationships. Although not generally provided, income statements reflecting functional and behavioral as well as natural expense classifications in sufficient detail to permit inter-statement analysis would represent an important contribution to the fulfillment of this guideline.

The guideline of disclosure of significant relationships is involved in decisions with regard to summarization and the attendant aggregation. Excessive summarization may have the effect of "burying" relevant data. The problem has two facets, the informal one which involves presenting information at an appropriate level of aggregation to be useful for managers in decision making, and the formal one involving the inherent characteristics of the procedures used in analyzing and synthesizing data. In dealing with reports based upon aggregated data, care must be taken both in the process of aggregation and in the interpretation of the results. Of basic concern is the fact that many mathematical operations performed on aggregated data yield results different from those obtained when the same operations are performed on the unaggregated data and the results then aggregated in the same manner as before. As an example, the calculation of an average sales price as an unweighted mean of the averages in each sales territory will ordinarily yield a result that is not representative of the overall pricing policy because it relies on aggregates and ignores differences of volume experienced in the different territories.

While no definitive solution to this problem exists, these factors warrant careful study by accountants, particularly when highly aggregated data are used. At the minimum, the sensitivity of the aggregation and the procedures employed should be evaluated against the purpose of the report or statement if the accountant is truly to serve as a specialist in quantitative information.

Inclusion of Environmental Information

In the context of communication theory, "environmental information" is best considered as that which describes the conditions under which the data were collected and the message prepared, along with the sender's assumption as to intended use of the information. In accounting reports this requires that the circumstances and the methods used be disclosed if there can be any reasonable doubt about such matters in the mind of the recipient of the information.

It also requires that reports prepared for special uses be labeled as such and the purposes specified to avoid the false conclusion that they are appropriate for general use. These requirements have long been recognized in accounting practice to a considerable degree, but in the case of certain regulated industries the matter has been turned around with special requirements of regulatory authorities being regarded as "generally accepted accounting principles" for those industries. It would be better for statements prepared in conformity with such requirements but not in conformity with generally accepted accounting principles to be labeled "prepared as required by the XYZ commission, and not in conformity with generally accepted accounting principles."

Information may be relevant, verifiable, unbiased, and quantifiable, yet the setting in which it is presented and the background knowledge necessary for its proper interpretation may be critical for informed use. The determination of the context in which information should be presented is becoming a more explicit consideration as the quantity and timeliness of available data continue to grow. The context in which general purpose public financial reports are placed is usually well understood. Reports prepared for special purposes or isolated pieces of information present quite a different situation. In these cases it is incumbent upon the preparer of the information to structure the context in which it is to be received—even to the extent of giving relevant, although unrequested, information to make the informative report truly useful. Computer output in some cases is an extreme example of the need fcr context, for often the inquirer does not even know how to ask for the relevant information. This is perhaps analogous to an inquiry as to the cost of a unit of product. A proper response to this question requires more than a single dollar figure. Costs for different purposes may have to be presented if no further information is obtained. Thus, it is conceivable that computers may have to be programmed to respond with whole sets of data rather than just "the" single number requested.

Uniformity of Practice Within and Among Entities

Where various alternative methods of measuring an economic activity exist, it is important that the best available one be used uniformly within a firm, by different firms, and, to the extent practicable, by different industries. This uniformity refers to consistent classification and terminology as well as consistent measurement, and it requires precise meanings. This guideline is required in order to meet a basic need of managers, investors, and creditors to compare results and financial conditions of different segments of firms, different firms, and different industries. A wise allocation of investment funds is to some degree frustrated by arbitrary differences in accounting methods which give different results from the same underlying economic facts. Uniformity is needed in order to meet the standard of freedom from bias, since some methods introduce a mathematical or statistical bias, and undue availability of alternatives obviously opens the way for manipulation of the results to suit the purposes of those who control the reports. For example, in a period of rising prices use of the last-in, first-out inventory method results in reporting income that is lower than would be produced by certain other inventory methods; and, indeed, LIFO has been widely adopted for that very purpose because of the consequent deferral, perhaps indefinitely, of a portion of the taxes on income. Further, the choice of "pooling of interest" accounting rather than "purchase" accounting in mergers may be made because of management's desire to suppress a high rate or to inflate a low rate of reported earnings, or to avoid showing purchased goodwill in the subsequent financial statement.

Basically, the guideline of uniformity is necessary for effective communication. If terminology classification, or measurement methods differ among units in a firm, among firms in an industry, or among industries, the reader of accounting reports may be misled.

The guideline of uniformity of practice should not exclude the choice of the best method available. As with the other guidelines and the standards, there exist reasonable trade-off rates. The standard of relevance and the guideline of appropriateness to intended use may be so crucial in a given setting that a departure from uniformity of practice (with full disclosure) may be justified. On the other hand, uniformity should never be the justification for inappropriate information.

Consistency of Practice Through Time

Much of the accounting function involves measurements and the communication of measured data as they relate to points in time and various time segments. Individual measurements are often useful, but even greater utility may come from the observation of trends disclosed by examination of a series of reports. For accounting measurements to serve as indices to make possible useful analyses through time, the measurement and reporting practices must be consistently applied. This consistency should relate to basic concepts reflected in accounting abstractions such as the nature of business income as well as to the terminology and, perhaps to a lesser extent, to the format of reports.

It must be recognized that absolute compliance with uniformity and consistency guidelines could cause biased information to be reported as time passes and conditions change and thus prevent needed improvements in measurement and communication methods. This, of course, must not be allowed to happen. A sense of reason and good judgment should prevail to provide answers to problems caused by a degree of conflict among the several standards and guidelines.

CHAPTER III

ACCOUNTING INFORMATION FOR EXTERNAL USERS

Accounting information is the chief means of reducing the uncertainty under which external users act as well as a primary means of reporting on stewardship. Ideally, more should be known about what does and should affect their decisions. The decision models used are both diverse and complex.

Most decisions based on accounting information involve some kind of prediction. Common examples include forecasts of future earnings, of probable payment of debt, and of likely managerial effectiveness.

It is not necessary to know in detail the needs of all the diverse users of accounting information to prepare relevant reports for them for certain classes of information are relevant to many decisions. As more is learned about external users, however, and as their decision models are refined and become better known, accounting theory and practice will change.

Evidence of dissatisfaction with extant accounting practices abounds. A principal criticism relates to the deficiencies of historical cost as a basis of predicting future earnings, solvency, or overall managerial effectiveness. We find historical-cost information relevant but not adequate for all purposes. We accordingly recommend that current-cost information as well as historical-cost information should be reported. Detailed suggestions for implementing this recommendation through multi-column statements are set out in the Appendices.

In addition to our recommendation that multi-valued information be given and particularly that both historical and current-cost information be reported, we also recommend:

1. Greater recognition of executory contracts (provided the Chapter II standards are met).

2. Adoption, because of greater relevance, of the "purchase" as opposed to the "pooling of interests" concept in reflecting corporate combinations.

3. Wider recognition of discovery values and accretion.

4. Recognition of deferred income taxes where they are relevant.

5. More accurate reflection of depreciation and obsolescence than current practice permits.

6. Capitalization of costs (such as research and development) incurred to yield future benefits where such benefits can be measured.

THE METHOD OF DEVELOPMENT

The informational needs of external users are sufficiently distinguishable from those of internal users to warrant treatment in separate chapters. At the same time, the four basic standards set out on the first page of Chapter II, and the statement made there that the utility of information lies in its ability to reduce uncertainty, apply with equal force to the needs of external and internal users.

Accounting information is especially crucial to external users because this group would otherwise have to act under an extreme degree of uncertainty. Internal users have proximate contacts with the entity and know of many significant events as they transpire, and so do not have to rely as much on accounting information as do external users. Furthermore, the problem of communicating accounting information to external users is complex because they are a heterogeneous group with widely varying interests. The facts that different decisions and different decision-makers are involved and that many unverifiable and unquantifiable types of information are probably significant to them indicate that accounting can supply only some of the information needed by external users.

Because of the great value of accounting information to external users, and because we have some knowledge of many users' needs, it is possible to develop significant accounting information even though the precise and total needs of each user for each decision are unknown. This is so because even crudely measured and only generally appropriate information may be of considerable use to external users in view of their highly uncertain situation. It follows that it is not necessary to develop a detailed list of all user needs in advance. On the contrary, until much more is known of the behavioral characteristics of external users, accounting information must be developed from a broad and imprecise understanding of the informational needs of external users. When and as the results of fundamental research on the informational needs of external users bear fruit, the structure of accounting theory and reporting based upon it can logically be expected to expand.

IDENTIFICATION OF EXTERNAL USERS

External users include present and potential investors, creditors, employees, stock exchanges, governmental units, customers, and others. Representatives of these users, such as security analysts, trade associations, credit rating bureaus, and trade union officers are also included.

Some external users of accounting information, such as regulatory commissions and tax authorities, not only have special needs but also the power to specify the information to be submitted. Although these users are not the major concern of this discussion, the committee believes that improvements suggested in this statement could well lead to more reliance on general purpose reports and fewer requirements for special formulations.

NATURE OF THE JUDGMENTS AND DECISIONS MADE BY EXTERNAL USERS

Those external users who have or contemplate having a direct relationship with an enterprise must decide, on the basis of all available information, whether to affiliate with or to modify an existing relationship with the firm. Investors and prospective investors must decide whether to buy or sell, or to retain their holdings. Suppliers must decide about lines of credit to be made available to the firm. Credit grantors must decide whether to make loans to the firm, what security or terms to require or, in the case of an existing commitment, whether to increase or decrease the loans or to require payment in full at maturity. Employees and prospective creditors must decide whether the goals of the firm are compatible with their own, whether the firm has prospects of stability or growth attractive to them, whether under existing agreements they are entitled to bonuses or other special compensation.

Other external users have informational needs that are not directly related to the commitment of personal or financial resources. Stock exchanges, for example, desire information adequate for the guidance of investors; this, in turn, embraces many of the informational needs of other external users. Information is also needed to determine whether standards for admission to listing on the stock exchange are met. Governmental units, including regulatory bodies, are interested in financial and statistical information to assist in making policy decisions. Trade associations have similar needs for information for broad policy decisions and for summarization and transmittal to their members. All these decisions, if not based upon sound accounting processes, can be seriously damaging to society as a whole.

Customers may also properly be concerned with such matters as the ability of a company to produce a product of an assured quality at an economical price or to service or replace equipment of special design. In those situations where customers contract to buy major amounts of products or services over long periods of time, their relationship takes on the characteristics of that of a creditor. In other cases, customer interests may be only indirect and may be implemented only through governmental regulation of trade and prices.

Many external users are concerned with one or more of the dimensions of stewardship. These range from the most elemental level of custodianship to responsibility for acquisition, utilization, and disposition of resources embracing the whole scope of management functions in a business entity. In this broad scope of concern, there is a correspondingly broad spectrum of judgments and decisions to be made.

At the most elemental level of stewardship responsibility it may be adequate to report only the kinds or numbers of resources received and disposed of, as might a custodian of securities, or the executor of an estate reporting on the distribution of property in kind. As the size and complexity of the resources administered increase and managerial responsibilities expand correspondingly, the need for variety in information emerges. Questions must be answered regarding the efficiency of administration of a profit-making enterprise or of its segments, and of effectiveness and efficiency in the use of resources to accomplish programmed goals. Similar questions arise with respect to stewardship in charitable and governmental organizations. Concern for the prudence of decisions made to retain or to sell assets in the light of available alternatives also is involved.

It is not the function of the accountant to dictate the decision models for users of accounting information. However, to the extent that there is a consensus with regard to all or part of a specific decision model, the accountant should select, process, and report relevant data. In those areas where the decision models used are less well known, the accountant should strive to provide information that is versatile and flexible. He should also respond to requests for specific information believed relevant by the user by giving such information as meets the suggested standards and by avoiding, or offering only with an appropriate caveat, information that fails to meet the standards or which meets them only to an unsatisfactory degree.

In seeking to provide information for external users, the accountant is accustomed to situations in which no specific requests for information are made, and in which responsibility for generalizations about the more important needs of users must be assumed jointly by the accountant and the entity whose activities are being reported upon. In view of this circumstance the committee advocates the reporting of all information that is believed to be relevant to the judgments and decisions of any substantial group of users. The committee is of the opinion that no single concept of value will suffice to fulfill this requirement, and thus concludes that multiple measurements should be reported in general purpose statements to meet a reasonably wide range of needs. (In this connection, see the comments in the section of this chapter headed "General Recommendations" and the illustrative statements given in Appendix B of this statement.)

EXTERNAL USES OF ACCOUNTING INFORMATION

The identification of many of the various external users of accounting information and some of the decisions and judgments they make permits some generalization regarding the uses to which this information may be put. These uses are necessarily stated only in general terms, because, as pointed out above, the decisions of users cannot be described in terms of fully known and detailed decision models.

Many persons use accounting information as an aid to some kind of prediction. We accordingly point out some of the more important efforts at prediction for which accounting information is considered particularly relevant. It is important to emphasize that accountants (with good justification) have avoided the role of forecasters in connection with reports to external users. The committee suggests that accounting information for external users should reflect their needs by reporting measurements and formulations thought to be relevant in the making of forecasts without implying that the information supplied is wholly adequate for such prediction.

Earnings

Almost all external users of financial information reported by a profit-oriented firm are involved in efforts to predict the earnings of the firm for some future period. Such predictions are most crucial in the case of present and prospective equity investors and their representatives—considered by many to be the most important of the user groups. Future earnings are the chief determinant of future dividends and future market prices of shares (given some predetermined price-earnings ratio), which, when taken together, are generally considered to provide the primary basis for establishing a subjective value for the shares in the mind of the user.[1] The past earnings of the firm

1. At this juncture we should point out that, so far as is known today, if investors (both potential and actual and both owners and creditors) could predict the amount and timing of future cash receipts from their investments then according to many theorists they should need little else in the way of information. It is fairly easy to generalize about such an unattainable ideal as knowledge of future cash receipts. Since future cash receipts cannot ordinarily be known exactly the parameters of the decision model have been broadened and it is quite difficult to specify what information is ideal.

are considered to be the most important single item of information relevant to the prediction of future earnings. It follows from this that past earnings should be measured and disclosed in such a manner as to give a user as much aid as practicable in efforts to make this prediction with a minimum of uncertainty.

This prediction is obviously much more than the simple extrapolation of past trends. Presumably, prediction of future earnings should consider predicted changes in environmental influences, such as predicted changes in the action of competitors resulting in changes in physical volume and price, as well as other influences affecting demand for one or more of the firm's products. Changes in prices of inputs must be considered, involving a host of assumptions regarding future economic conditions, external and internal to the firm. This is a hazardous activity even for the most sophisticated analyst.

A person using financial statements as an aid in predicting future earnings has a right to demand from the accountant measurements of past earnings that supply as much relevant information as possible.

Financial Position and Liquidity

To some users efforts to predict future financial position and debt-paying power may be of greater importance than prediction of earnings. This is especially true in the cases of short-term creditors, who must assess the uncertainty inherent in near-future repayment of debt. It may also be true for customers and employees. Predictions of longer term financial position are more closely related to predictions of earnings, so that neither can be accomplished independently of the other. Again, such efforts cannot be wisely undertaken without concurrent consideration of certain uncontrollable environmental factors, such as the expected cost of maintenance of productive capacity and prospective tax and interest rates, as well as internal factors such as plans for growth, dividend policy, and methods of financing. Statements of cash and working-capital flows covering past periods may be useful in making these predictions provided due regard is given to such factors as (a) the repetitive or non-repetitive nature of various classes of transactions, and (b) the influence that changes in managerial policy and environmental factors may have. Prediction of financial position and asset liquidity by creditors and others may be an even more difficult activity than prediction of earnings, and the accountant must be particularly sensitive to these difficulties in providing assistance by reporting as much relevant information on financial position, funds flows, and earnings of past periods as possible.

Prediction of financial position and liquidity may also be important to users of financial information reported by non-profit entities. Such prediction made by the external users is subject to many of the difficulties surrounding the profit-oriented firm with the added difficulty imposed by the absence of the management objective of long-run profitability. Even in such cases, careful distinction between recurring and non-recurring classifications of transactions in statements of cash flows and funds flows covering past periods may be relevant to the prediction of future financial position. Of much greater assistance in such predictions are statements of budgeted cash flows occasionally distributed to external users of information of non-profit entities, provided such statements meet the tests of verifiability and freedom from bias.

Management Effectiveness

Efforts of external users to predict the effectiveness of the management in future periods cannot be disassociated from the predictions of earnings and predictions of financial position and liquidity discussed above. The prediction of such effectiveness would appear to be highly important to virtually all groups of external users of accounting information and is not the special interest of any particular group. On the other hand, prediction of future management effectiveness is not identical with prediction of earnings and financial position, and in fact may be considered as one of the most difficult elements in the prediction process. Financial statements covering past periods provide the most important quantitative information relevant to this prediction, and the relevance of this information depends in large measure on the separation of the results within management's control from those outside management's control. This suggests that the effect of uncontrollable environmental factors on earnings or financial position should be identified and distinguished to the extent possible from those factors reflecting the actions of the current management. It also suggests that the current management should not be charged (or credited) with the financial effects of actions taken by previous managements. It implies that the effectiveness of management must be assessed in terms of specified time periods if meaningful comparisons with other periods are to be drawn.

Stewardship

Highly varied relationships exist in society in which one party entrusts resources to another. These range from a simple custodianship in which the specific asset is to be returned intact, to a donor-donee relation in which the donor expects no material return but may require a report of use and effectiveness. Within these extremes lies the familiar investment of funds for profit by either a creditor or a proprietor. Seldom if ever are economic resources entrusted by one person or entity to another without the expectation of an accounting for the resources; even the donor of an X-ray machine to a hospital may request a report of the number of cases served. Notwithstanding the great diversity of information involved, the accountant is increasingly expected to be a major processor of information in these relationships. In some cases the informational needs are too simple to warrant specific attention here; in others, such as the specific informational needs of customers looking to the entity as a major source of supply, the measures are not as yet entirely clear and are merely mentioned in this statement.

Accountants can prepare meaningful reports of stewardship only to the extent that they are aware of or can postulate accurately the provisions of the agreement between the parties to the stewardship arrangement. In the many cases of external reporting, the parties themselves (i.e., the external users) are not clear on the nature or extent of the responsibility delegated; thus the accountant finds that he must impute some relationship between the entity and the users, and from this draw conclusions as to what information is relevant to the users' needs.

The latter point is illustrated by the reporting of cash receipts and disbursements that has become customary for many not-for-profit entities, without giving any clear indication that the responsibility of the entity is limited to administration or custody of the cash assets or both. If the entity is to be held responsible for efficient administration, periodic reporting on an accrual basis would be required. For example, taxes receivable, with adjustment for possible uncollectibles, should be reported if the entity has responsibility for levying and collecting taxes. Measurements in current terms of resources entrusted to not-for-profit entities are relevant primarily for choosing between alternatives in the acquisition, maintenance, and disposition of such non-cash assets.

Comment on External Uses of Accounting Information

We note that as more is learned about the actual decision-making process, and, further, as the decision-making process itself changes, modification in the information presented by accountants will be needed. The fact that decision models are often complex, that they may change as conditions and attitudes change and thereby take on forms different from traditional concepts, may be illustrated by the case of automobile pricing in this country immediately after World War II. It is well known that automobile manufacturers in the United States did not maximize their short-run profits immediately after World War II when they faced a seller's market, as an ordinary interpretation of economic theory would assume. The explanation is, of course, that consideration of the long-run effects on public opinion and possible political or regulatory reactions to such a policy led to restraint, so that new automobiles were rationed by other means than the price system (insofar as the manufacturer was concerned). Again, it is well known now that businessmen do not act on the premises of ordinary economic theory alone in deciding whether or not to make corporate contributions to charity or even on the question of continuing or winding up a business.

Similar modifications in our understanding of the decision models of the external users of accounting information may be made in the future. Any changes are readily accommodated by the accounting standards advocated in Chapter II; it is essential in their application only that we know whether or not certain information is relevant to a particular class of decisions (assuming satisfactory conformance to the other standards) and not that we be able to specify the model in detail.

THE STANDARDS AND EXTERNAL USERS

From the viewpoint of the external user, it is essential that accounting information be relevant to his needs. The accountant, in developing the most useful information, must sometimes sacrifice a degree of relevance in order to meet the standards of verifiability, freedom from bias, and quantifiability.

Only a very limited amount of relevant accounting information can meet completely the standard of verifiability in the sense of a complete statistical consensus. For example, even statistically determined allowances for uncollectible receivables, pension liabilities, and certain other liabilities, such as those for product guarantees, are estimates that typically have well below 100 percent certainty. Other predictions such as those implicit in the depreciation of long-lived assets are not completely verifiable even though they are widely accepted. Accountants generally refrain from reporting budgets relating to future periods to external users, on the ground that the information is not sufficiently verifiable, although it might be highly relevant to external user's needs. Failure to observe the standard of verifiability to a minimum degree would place the accountant, in some cases, in the role of forecaster and would reduce the confidence of the user and thereby diminish the usefulness of accounting reports. We believe that a substantial level of verifiability is most important for externally reported accounting information.

The question of verifiability is especially important in relation to the use of current-cost valuation. Accountants can report current-cost valuations, in addition to original-transaction based information, in financial statements only if all representations can be verified to an acceptable degree. A point frequently overlooked in the "cost vs. value" controversy in accounting is the fact that verifiability of evidence supporting a measurement can be widely different depending upon the nature of the particular asset, the use made of it, and the economic circumstances in which it is found. In this regard, current cost does not differ from historical cost which must be amortized on the basis of various estimates of life. To hold that the general practice of valuing assets at "current cost" for accounting purposes is not acceptable because *some* estimates of current cost are not verifiable is an untenable position. To say that the current-cost estimate of an asset in a given situation is not verifiable is simply to say that there is insufficient evidence to warrant recognition that the value of the asset has changed. If evidence concerning the current cost of certain assets is not verifiable, this should not mitigate against current costs that are verifiable. Furthermore, the original-transaction data or other valuation will continue to be reported in the current-cost column where current cost is unverifiable because there is no other evidence which meets the minimum requirement of the verifiability standard. Financial reports to external users may appropriately include in the current-cost column some assets stated at recently determined "current cost," other assets at older estimates of "current cost," and still others at original-transaction price, where verifiability of the different kinds of information varies among the assets.

The degree of verifiability of historical transaction-based valuations may be extremely high, and some sacrifice of verifiability for increased relevance may improve the usefulness of the information. In some instances, the use of current cost for assets, such as securities, may involve no sacrifice of verifiability.

The next attribute which the accountant requires of accounting information for external users is that the information meets at least a minimum level of the standard of freedom from bias. Of course, the standard of verifiability tends to exclude certain kinds of personal bias that otherwise might creep into financial reporting, but there normally remains considerable opportunity for bias to exist in financial reports. For example, the continued use of historical-cost valuations during and following periods of inflation will tend to understate assets and overstate earnings as compared with the experience of firms acquiring the same assets more recently. In such a situation, year-to-year comparisons for a single firm will tend to show improvement that may be illusory. Aside from inflation, the influence of the income tax law and general "conservatism" will often result in an understatement of assets and "premature" expense recognition. Also, the influence of management on financial representations to external users may produce bias, since corporate management is naturally interested in representing itself to outsiders in as favorable a light as is possible.

Current-cost valuations can contribute to the elimination of such biases, particularly if accountants take responsibility for the measurement methods used in developing the accounting information. Reporting the current cost, less depreciation, of plant and equipment items, for instance, will tend to nullify the influence of "too fast" depreciation methods. Reporting multiple valuations of an asset will reduce the pressure on a single valuation to serve many purposes.

The final attribute, after relevance, required by the information developer before a measure of activities can be considered significant to external users is that it meets the standard of quantifiability. In the main, accountants have traditionally required that accounting information to external users have a single valuation, for example, that advertising expense is $18,121, no more and no less. In some instances there has been an implication of a possible range of values, as when receivables are reported at their face amounts less a valuation contra, but this implication usually goes unnoticed. Because the accuracy of many accounting measurements depends upon future activity, there is no compelling reason why the accountant should not report in terms of interval estimates or probability distributions. For example, advertising expense might be reported as within the range of $10,400 to $18,121 depending on the probability that all of a campaign costing $7,721 has asset status at the reporting date—a zero probability would assign no asset value and state advertising at $18,121. In other words, it may be that accountants usually have required too narrow a view of compliance with the standard of quantifiability.

The need for meaningful quantification of many relevant factors exists in both profit-oriented and not-for-profit entities. External users may wish to know degrees of employee morale, customer satisfaction, product quality, and reputation of a given entity. If quantification of these were possible, a substantial amount of additional relevant information could be provided the external users. The accountant must constantly be alert to the possible applications of new measurement methods to develop additional quantifiable information for external users.

The absence of meaningful quantification techniques is more apparent in the not-for-profit area. Much remains to be done in developing measures of performance here.

Appendix A discusses means of satisfying the standards for accounting information with regard to current-cost valuation, and Appendix B illustrates the results which obtain when accounting information for external purposes is reported in terms of current costs along with historical-cost information in the traditional statements.

GENERAL RECOMMENDATIONS

Accounting does not now fulfill all the requirements that are made of it. This is evidenced by (1) a growing body of accounting, financial, and economic literature in which criticism of and controversies over accounting information are common; (2) the research efforts of organizations such as the American Accounting Association, the American Institute of Certified Public Accountants, the Financial Executives Institute, the National Association of Accountants, societies of financial analysts, and others seeking to improve accounting information; and (3) the increasing concern of governmental bodies, stock exchanges, and other groups with the adequacy of accounting information. These writings and activities call our attention to a number of needs that should be considered, and we use them as a source of subjects to which we wish to address ourselves. We feel that the problem areas discussed below are of crucial importance, but are not necessarily exhaustive of the problems facing accounting today, and much less a prescription of the boundaries of the accounting function of the future.

A substantial part of the criticism of accounting is concerned with the limitations of historical transaction-based data to serve a significant number of desired uses. At the same time, the proposed replacement of historical transaction-based information by current values (however defined) fails to satisfy a number of other uses. Our standards provide an approach to the solution of this conflict. Historical transaction-based information has been verified by a market transaction, and hence is of great usefulness when verifiability is emphasized. Current values, on the other hand, reflect not only the transactions of the firm but also the impact of the environment on the firm beyond the completed transactions. Thus they possess a high degree of relevance for many uses in which prediction is prominent. The presentation of the historical information alone excludes the full impact of the environment on the firm; presentation of current cost information alone obscures the record of consummated market transactions. The committee recommends that both kinds of information be presented in a multi-valued report, in which the two kinds of information appear in adjacent columns. This has the added advantage of revealing the impact of environmental changes, since the historical information reflects market transactions, the current-cost information reflects market transactions plus "unrealized" market influences, and the difference shows the effect of unrealized environmental influences. Inclusion of the environmental information in what is reported better enables the accountant to meet the standard of relevance.

In addition to presenting accounting information on more than one basis, the diversity of uses and the lack of prior knowledge of the decision models involved indicate the desirability of a method of reporting that permits use of detailed information that has the potential for satisfying many different informational needs. This suggests that separate elements of an income computation, for example, which have significance for predicting or analyzing different functions, should be observable in the statements. Long established practice in the United States, for example, has recognized this principle in income statements that disclose cost of goods sold, selling expenses, and other elements that respond individually to distinct forces. Extension of this principle should be made wherever possible to reveal other relationships. For example, it would be helpful to external users to have (1) separation of expenses into fixed and variable, or controllable and non-controllable elements (as is often done internally), and (2) separation of revenues, costs or expenses, and assets by product or divisional lines.

Means of expressing accounting information on a current basis which meet the standards of verifiability, freedom from bias, and quantifiability are suggested in Appendix A of this statement. The current basis recommended is current cost of replacement of the services represented in the resources and commitments of the entity. Illustrative statements which embody the recommendations of the committee are given in Appendix B of this statement. It is to be noted that the statements are offered as illustrations and are not intended to be definitive in all details. The statements distinguish between changes in current replacement costs *per se* and changes in expression of dollar amounts required by changes in the general purchasing power of money.

ADDITIONAL SPECIFIC RECOMMENDATIONS

Our recommendations on certain prominent problems of accounting are set out on the next pages.

I. *The presentation of multi-valued information.* Because of the importance of the issue we emphasize once more the general recommendation for reporting both historical and current costs. Historical cost has often been criticized for its low predictive potential for many decisions, and for the bias such information contains when taken to represent a description of current wealth. However, the record based upon historical costs has a high degree of verifiability and lack of personal bias since the information is derived from completed market transactions. By the same token, quantifiability is usually made simple and direct by the terms of most contracts. Such information therefore has special merit where verifiability and quantifiability are paramount, as in fiduciary relationships, for example. In those cases where legal rules contemplate the use of historical cost it has a relevance of a special type. Historical-cost information has relevance also in the appraisal of management and hence organizational performance over time, since it records discernible trends.

The reporting of both historical and current-cost information, as here recommended, increases the usefulness of the whole report. Such reporting tends to remove the objections to historical cost which flow from attempts to use it for purposes to which it is not suited.

II. *Executory contracts.* Accounting at present recognizes most market transactions involving goods, services, or money as one of the elements of the transaction. Present accounting also generally ignores, except in special circumstances, transactions involving an exchange of a promise for a promise. Leases, purchase commitments, executive and other labor contracts are generally denied recognition until the services or goods specified in the contract are either used, delivered, or paid for.

Many of these contracts meet the standards of verifiability, freedom from bias, and quantifiability at least as well as other reported events.

Generally a contract specifies amounts that allow verification and quantification. For contracts of long duration, a valuation problem in terms of present values exists, but this problem is no greater than in other problems involving accounting judgment, such as estimation of collectibility of receivables. These contracts also do not appear to contain any biases. The only reason for exclusion, where the other standards are met, must be based on relevance. The committee feels that short-term contracts or contracts that are essentially renewed periodically in equal amounts may justifiably be ignored on the grounds that information about such commitments does not possess sufficient relevance to justify inclusion in accounting reports. Perhaps a better way of stating the above conclusion is that in such cases deferring recognition of such events until the services or goods are used or delivered does not do much harm. This, however, cannot be said about contracts extending over long periods that are material or that are not repetitive. Information about such contracts is clearly relevant to a host of decisions involving stewardship, changes in management, credit extension, and investment decisions. Recording of these events would also result in greater uniformity of reporting essentially similar events where the only difference lies in the form of obligation assumed. Therefore, the committee recommends the reporting of all long-term leases, material and non-repetitive purchase commitments, pension plans, and executive compensation contracts including stock options or deferred payments and the like in dollar terms in the regular framework of the statements.

This does not imply that all useful accounting information must be incorporated in the double-entry structure; at the same time, maximizing what is recorded in that system is a useful means of avoiding errors of omission in reporting of relevant information.

III. *Purchase and pooling.* Although market transactions resulting in combinations or reorganizations of business entities are recorded, there is considerable freedom in recording such transactions as either a pooling of interests (where the market transaction is treated as if it created no *new* exchange values for the assets involved) or as a purchase (where new exchange values resulting from the market transaction are recognized). This is perhaps the classic case of quantifiability and verifiability warring with relevance. It is true that carrying forward the existing book values of the two combining entities is eminently quantifiable since the figures exist on the books. It is more than questionable that such a treatment, which essentially ignores the new exchange values created by a significant market transaction such as the combination of two companies, can be said to be relevant for investment decisions. When a single machine is purchased, the book value of that machine on the seller's books is considered irrelevant for the purchaser's records. The same is true when a company is merged or purchased. The committee feels that in most instances in such a transaction enough evidence exists to provide verifiability and freedom from bias, and that relevant exchange values resulting from such transactions should be recognized, and thus recommends that the pooling of interest technique be disallowed.

IV. *Current costs.* Our earlier discussion has emphasized the importance of multi-valued reporting. For emphasis, we give further attention to current costs here. Accounting in most countries has up to now not recognized general environmental changes (e.g., inflation) and has ordinarily recognized specific environmental changes (e.g., a change in the price of tires) only when resulting in diminution of assets. The committee feels that certain general and specific environmental changes meet the standards laid down in Chapter II to a sufficient degree to warrant recognition in the accounting reports.

Ideally, the investor would like to know the present value of the future net receipts on his investment. This would require knowledge of the flow of receipts and disbursements of the enterprise over the life of the unit. In actuality such data cannot be predicted with as much accuracy as most persons would like. It seems clear, however, that information about the effect of specific environmental changes, i.e., specific price changes affecting the enterprise, would be useful and relevant in better predicting such flows and therefore in making investment decisions. Further, separating general from specific changes improves the estimates. The committee realizes that making such estimates requires much information and does not suggest that current-cost information is the only relevant variable, but only that it *is* a relevant variable. Since we advocate multiple-value accounting, we do not have to establish that current cost is the only relevant measure, but if it meets the other standards, few could deny that it is useful. We therefore recommend that current costs be reported. There are many approaches to "current values," and we suggest that the approach that is most likely to meet the standards of accounting information proposed in Chapter II of this statement is current cost to replace the assets or services involved. Means of calculating such costs are discussed in Appendix A of this statement.

V. *Discovery values.* The standard of relevance requires that discovery values and the value of timber growth and similar resources on a current-cost-equivalent basis be reported. Means of calculating a current-cost figure for these assets are discussed in Appendix A.

VI. *Recognition of deferred taxes.* The recognition of deferred taxes arising from the use of current costs has relevance to the prediction of cash flows in connection with depreciable assets. This fact follows from the circumstances that the increases to current cost are not deductible for tax purposes in the kind of income tax system used in the United States, which means that the tax outlays of the firm recognizing an increase in costs will exceed those of a firm buying the same assets at the same current-cost figures. In the case of deferred taxes arising from a discrepancy between depreciation rates used in the general accounts and in the tax returns, the relevance of deferred taxes for inter-firm comparisons is less clear. It is possible that the differences between book and tax bases may have relevance for inter-period predictions of a given firm. This is a problem requiring further analysis. The clear justification for the amounts added to show current costs is the basis for the inclusion of deferred taxes on this increase in the illustrative statements given in Appendix B. Because of the need for inter-firm comparisons of asset amounts and for measures of asset changes over time, and because the deferred income tax is peculiar to the experience of each firm, the deferred tax has been shown on the right side of the balance sheet in Appendix B, and not as a contra-asset account.

VII. *Depreciation and obsolescence.* If information about depreciation is to have maximum relevance to user needs it must be co-ordinated with revenue from the assets being depreciated. The committee deplores the tendency to design depreciation calculations to compensate for a failure to recognize current cost levels. It also regrets the tendency to report to stockholders depreciation that has been accelerated beyond any realistic estimate of useful life of assets in order to achieve a tax advantage or to manipulate income calculations. It is hoped that multi-dimensional reporting as recommended here will lessen the incentive to design depreciation calculations for those purposes. Obsolescence, to the extent it can be quantified by equipment replacement studies or similar means, should be recognized explicitly and regularly.

VIII. *Conversions.* A conversion is a recombination of asset services reflecting the production of new utility. Expenditures and other costs devoted to such activities as research and development, personnel recruitment and training, and marketing campaigns often involve an element of future usefulness and are examples of conversions that would be recognized if quantifiable and verifiable. Present practice recognizes such costs as assets and hence as conversion of cash and services to new asset status only when a physical product or such a legal privilege as a patent results. When practice refuses to recognize the conversion to asset status by assigning a zero value to the asset it assigns all the expenditure to the expense category, thus presenting an expense that is equally unverifiable as deserving expense status. This result is somewhat curious in view of a popular emphasis upon the income statement but understandable in terms of the tendency to conservatism in asset valuation. Relevance demands that the best available techniques for allocating these expenditures to asset and expense categories should be utilized. Decision models used by management are becoming more explicit and should be availed of for this purpose. Studies that quantify the future benefits of advertising and of research expenditures are becoming more prevalent, and where applicable should be used.

CHAPTER IV

ACCOUNTING INFORMATION FOR INTERNAL MANAGEMENT

Accounting for external users has generally received more attention in the literature than has accounting for internal management. In addition, the theory of management itself has, until recently, provided little guidance for management accountants. As a consequence, management accounting is less well developed and the foundations for it are less well understood than is the case with externally oriented accounting theory.

There has been, however, increased attention devoted to this area in recent years and a definition of managment accounting formulated by the 1958 AAA Committee on Management Accounting is analyzed and used as the expository base for beginning this chapter. For it, management accounting was "the application of appropriate techniques and concepts in processing the historical and projected economic data of an entity to assist management in establishing plans for reasonable economic objectives and in the making of rational decisions with a view toward achieving these objectives."

While theories of management differ, the two principal functions of management are generally considered to be those of *planning* and *control*. These functions are analyzed to provide a background for discussing the informational needs of management. Planning is primarily a decision-making activity involving selection of alternatives. Control ensures that the plans are executed. Their informational requirements are often different and the accounting system should be responsive to the needs of both functions.

In fulfilling management's informational requirements, the standards for accounting information recommended in Chapter II are applied. Some variation in conformance with these standards, compared with those required in the case of external reporting, is apparent because of the unique position of internal management and the differing end uses to which the information is put.

Management's needs for accounting information are examined from the standpoint of (a) information provided by the conventional accounting system model, and (b) information provided separately from this model. (It should be noted that this dichotomy is used only for expository purposes as the committee strongly advocates a unified accounting information system.) From this examination, two points emerge.

First, the conventional model, through the correspondence of its output with the profit objective and determination of financial position serves the function of overall management control very well. Forecasts of the future can be made by examining its output over time.

37

Through proper structuring, the conventional model can yield highly useful data on a responsibility basis. Its deficiencies are most notable in respect to planning and the evaluation of managerial alternatives.

Second, in serving management's requirements for relevant information the accountant should go beyond both the conventional model and historically-valued transaction data. Fruitful areas of extension include cost behavior analysis; use of time-adjusted cash flow projections; the reporting of projected alternatives by use of ranges or probability distributions rather than single-valued estimates; and the development and manipulation of inventory and other management models and simulation techniques.

INTRODUCTION

Statement of the Problem

The objective of accounting for internal use is to provide information to persons within an organization that enables them to make informed judgments and effective decisions which further the organization's goals. These judgments and decisions relate to a large and widely varied collection of issues and problems, and the information needed for their proper resolution is extensive and enormously diverse in nature and in classification.

A large part, but not all, of the information needed by management comes through the accounting system. Some of this information has the same basic nature as that incorporated into the organization's financial statements but is presented at a level of greater detail and with possible modifications in the nature and level of classification. Other information lies outside of the external financial reporting framework yet is a fundamental part of the internal accounting process. Both types of accounting information are considered in this chapter.

Accounting theory has evidenced relatively less concern for the managerial area. This is perhaps natural as accounting is a practical discipline and there has been, in the past, little theoretical guidance from the management literature. The developing theory of management, however, is now providing more structure for evaluating the information needed. This, in combination with the increased requirements for quantified information structured to meet a variety of explicit needs has prompted the committee to include in a statement of accounting theory a chapter on accounting for internal management and, in particular, to concern itself with examining the nature and characteristics of management's needs.

Method of Analysis

It is appropriate to begin by examining the nature of accounting for internal management and the concept of management accounting. Such an examination requires an understanding of the management function which the accounting system serves. While principles of accounting for external use are, at least to date, based upon the economic concepts of income and wealth, principles of accounting for internal use are based not only upon economic concepts but also upon considerations arising from the growing body of knowledge which is rapidly gaining recognition as a theory of management. Thus an examination of the management function is in order to enable us to understand the informational needs of managers and to then relate these needs to the standards for accounting information.

Since the theory of management is not as developed as the theory of economics, the relatively tight, logical relationships that exist between the standards of accounting information and the reports prepared for external use cannot always be obtained in internal reporting. The standards are applicable, nonetheless, and the relationships between them and internal accounting information are discussed following the investigation of the informational needs of managers. The last section of the chapter considers the subject matter of the accounting system that lies within and without the external reporting framework.

THE CONCEPT OF MANAGEMENT ACCOUNTING

The objective of internal accounting is to serve management. In order to understand the effect of this objective on internal accounting, it is useful to examine the concepts and implications contained in the following definition:

> Management accounting is the application of appropriate techniques and concepts in processing the historical and projected economic data of an entity to assist management in establishing plans for reasonable economic objectives and in

the making of rational decisions with a view toward achieving these objectives.[1]

"The Application of Appropriate Techniques and Concepts"

This definition provides no specific restrictions to the scope of the accounting function. Indeed, rather than being constrained by traditions which reflect a different and less highly developed management technology, the accounting system is charged with responding to the informational requirements of managers through the problems they meet and the solution techniques they use.

Fulfilling these requirements places two responsibilities upon the accountant. The first is that of utilizing the most appropriate technology available to produce the information needed. The second is providing this information in a form that is relevant to the problem requirements and with characteristics compatible with the methodology used in solving the problem.

The breadth of management's scope and hence the requirements placed on information involve the management accountant not only in his own technology and in economics but in the behavioral and management sciences areas as well. Management is increasingly involved in using quantified data in areas where qualitative judgment prevailed a decade or two ago. When this requires measures and techniques based on other disciplines, the management accountant must be prepared to fulfill these needs. He should understand the information requirements well enough to be an intelligent supplier of relevant data for use in the decision-making models if, indeed, not the originator and manipulator of these models. At the minimum, the accounting system must provide the means to evaluate the appropriateness of the information needed and in no case should the accountant be merely the passive supplier of untreated data.

The precise limits of management accounting and the extent to which its technology will expand are not readily determinable at this point in its development. There is no logical reason, however, why management accounting should be constrained by external reporting conventions of a past era. Neither should internal reporting be conditioned by the nature of the accountant's obligations to third parties or society in

---

1. Adapted from the report of the 1958 Committee on Management Accounting, **The Accounting Review,** April 1959, p. 210.

general except, of course, that the results arising from the decisions made using internal accounting information require disclosure and control—including such controls as may be required by social considerations.

"Historical and Projected"

The definition of management accounting refers to historical and projected data. The inclusion of projections within the scope of management accounting is fundamental and indeed is implied by the explanation and evaluation of alternatives as well as the bringing of new alternatives into view. This inclusion does not necessarily distinguish management accounting from external reporting and the two are in no way incompatible if accounting is well performed. But the use by accountants of projections and forecasts, as in the analysis of hypothetical possibilities as alternatives, is, at present at least, of greater importance and propriety in serving the needs of managers than in fulfilling the external reporting role.

"Economic Data"

The definition next refers to economic data. Internal accounting deals with economic measures which are often, but not always, stated in financial or monetary forms. Budget and control reports, while almost always stated in dollar terms at plant and company-wide levels, are often useful for their intended purpose at the shop level in physical terms—without the application of dollar multipliers. In addition, analytical tools that have become commonplace in management require data in various non-dollar forms. Programming models require measurements representing capacity limitations, product interdependencies, rates of output, efficiency determinations for alternative output levels, and other data of economic significance but non-financial in expression. The tendency toward integration of information systems within the entity adds a further important dimension to these requirements and hence to the necessity for the accountant to increase his capacity for dealing with economic data in their broadest connotations. Indeed, this problem is a crucial one and is examined in a later section. It is important to recognize at this point that it is increasingly difficult for the accountant to accept responsibility for one set of financial data without becoming involved with a larger and larger share of the organization's information function.

"Assist Management"

The definition charges management accounting to assist management. This emphasizes the service role of accounting in providing information for managerial decisions and monitoring their implementation. It is important to distinguish between the information function (accounting) and the management decision function. While increasingly interrelated, these functions nonetheless have basic differences in their objectives, scope, and responsibilities. Further, their separation obviates the situation of a function supplying data which conditions its own actions and then being the major, if not sole, appraiser of its own performance. The loss of objectivity in such a case is obvious.

Objective or not, full utilization of the services of management accounting and the skills of the management accountant often requires the participation of the accountant as an integral member of the management team. This is of increasing importance as the expansion of management technology, information processing capabilities, and the integration of the information function all tend to make the demarcation between the information function and the decision function less and less clear. A factor which mitigates this loss of objectivity is the increase in the knowledge of the accountant of the informational requirements and the information system. This increased knowledge substitutes professional for personal judgment and reduces, operationally, the requirement separating the provider of the information from its analysis and use. While recognizing these forces and trends, and the ensuing problems and opportunities, the remainder of this chapter is concerned almost exclusively with the information function of accounting rather than the role of the accountant as a member of the management team.

"Establishing Plans . . . and Making Rational Decisions . . ."

Finally, the definition mentions ". . . establishing plans for reasonable economic objectives and in the making of rational decisions with a view toward achieving these objectives." This is an expression of the management functions which accounting serves and, while the management function and the requirements it places upon accounting are examined in the next two sections of this chapter, three implications of the definition should be noted here.

First, accounting not only aids in formulating plans and guiding decisions made to achieve objectives; it also assists in the setting of goals and in the evaluation of the reasonableness of the objectives themselves.

Second, economic considerations are inherent in almost all organizational activity taken to achieve goals whether these goals are economic or not. For reasons developed in Chapter I and elsewhere, the committee feels that accounting can be of use in both the establishment and attainment of non-economic objectives and goals.

Finally, the achievement of objectives involves not only planning but implementation and control. The control function is closely associated with accounting and a more complete discussion of this point is included in the later sections of this chapter.

THE MANAGEMENT FUNCTION

Concepts of Management

The process of management has been, over the years, the subject of a large and continually growing literature. The authors of these studies have examined management and the organizations in which it functions from a variety of points of view. The functions the managers perform have been classified by the authors in a number of different ways. The classifications, however, possess basic similarities—with the main differences stemming either from combining several functions into one (and vice versa) or from the particular point of view or emphasis taken by the analyst. Regardless of the different levels of functional aggregation, management is seen almost without exception as performing two basic functions of *planning* and *control*.[2]

A second way of viewing organizations examines the characteristics of the actions taken and the degree of structure available to guide them. This view divides activities into *programmed* and *unprogrammed* groups where the latter refers to those activities that are categorized as "novel, unstructured, and consequential."[3]

---

2. One of the earlier writers on modern management, Henri Fayol, stated that, ". . . to manage is to forecast and plan, to organize, to command, to coordinate, and to control." [**General and Industrial Management,** translated by Constance Storries (London: Sir Isaac Pitman and Sons, Ltd., 1949), pp. 5-6.] The distinctions between these concepts cannot be tightly drawn and some scholars have even postulated that management can be viewed solely in terms of decision making. Others have included planning and control but have added another function which has variously been called organizing, implementing, or coordinating.

3. Herbert A. Simon, **The New Science of Management Decisions** (New York: Harper and Brothers Publishers, 1960), p. 6. See also, James G. March and Herbert A. Simon, **Organizations** (New York: John Wiley and Sons, Inc., 1958).

Without attempting to be exhaustive or even complete with respect to the particular management frameworks cited, a two-dimensional classification can be developed using the concepts mentioned above. This classification can be used as a referent in examining the informational needs of management. This framework is expressed as follows:

Activity / Function	Unprogrammed	Programmed
Planning	(1)	(2)
Control	(3)	(4)

In this framework, top-level planning falls in Cell 1 while control of factory operations falls in Cell 4. The function of implementation can be viewed as planning programmed activities, Cell 2, or the control of unprogrammed activities, Cell 3.

The Planning Process

Planning involves making choices between alternatives and is primarily, if not entirely, a decision-making activity. The alternatives involved may be of different natures and at different levels of the decision-making hierarchy. At the highest levels the alternatives may be different organizational goals or objectives for the organization to attempt to accomplish. At lower levels decision making may involve alternative resource allocation programs to achieve a particular established sub-goal.

While these resource allocations can be considered as the implementation function, they can also be viewed as planning that takes place at a lower level in the organization with a different problem in mind. What the function is called is less important than the recognition that the selection of an alternative plan of action is not the end of the management function. Steps must also be taken to put the plan into action. These implementation steps can be viewed as a separate function or considered as part of the planning process but done on a lower, and perhaps more programmed, organizational level.

The planning function can be broken down into four stages, or elements, which may vary in importance with particular problem situations but which are present in some degree in all planning activities regardless of the scope of the problem involved or the characteristics of the subject matter under examination. These four elements are:

1. Recognizing and defining the problem.

2. Searching for alternative solutions.

3. Evaluating the alternative solutions.

4. Selecting an alternative based on the results of evaluation.

Each of these stages of the planning process requires information. These informational requirements are discussed in detail in a following section.

The Control Process

Control, the other management function, involves the process of ensuring that the alternatives chosen are accepted and the plans for implementing them are carried out. Further, control provides feedback on both the quality of the actions and the quality of the plans themselves. Thus it acts as an agent of change both upwards and downwards in the organization. That is, the control process permits and reports upon actions taken contrary to those which were planned but which were, nevertheless, more effective in achieving the organization's goals.

Control can also be considered to involve coordination—making sure that all aspects of an interrelated set of operations dovetail with each other—which includes such factors as the quantities produced, their timing, and their characteristics. This coordination can take place on high organizational levels, as in the case of divisional budgets, or lower down at the operational production level or shop floor.

In ensuring that the plans formulated are carried out, the control process is concerned with the performance of individuals involved in the planned activities. While this concern may turn to the motivations governing individual behavior, control usually involves structuring the environment so that the desired results can be achieved, and providing stimuli necessary to evoke and guide the desired actions. For programmed activities, this involves the selecting of the appropriate methods to be used in task performance, ensuring that this "program" is followed, and monitoring and reporting on the output or results.

For unprogrammed activities control is more difficult. Here, the methods are often unspecified, or unknown in advance, and it is difficult, if not impossibie, to assess intermediate methods or results on the way toward achievement of the specified plan. The problem is exemplified in the control of research and development where there are few guides for methodology and the nature of the goal is often relatively unknown. Indeed, management is in the position of having to control such an activity without knowing exactly what the activity should be doing. In these cases the environment is structured to permit flexibility of behavior; stimuli are provided in general rather than specific terms; and the results are reported for subsequent evaluation, but standards for comparison at the time of reporting are usually not available.

INFORMATION NEEDS OF MANAGEMENT

Information for Planning

The information required for planning is best examined in relation to the different stages of the planning process. In the previous section the stages were considered to be (1) recognizing and defining problems, (2) searching for alternative solutions, (3) evaluating the alternatives obtained, and (4) selecting among the evaluated alternatives.

Recognizing and defining the problem requires an information system that brings problems to the attention of management and then permits the particular conditions involved to be isolated and understood. The information leading to the recognition of problem situations often comes through the control system and is discussed in greater detail below. For defining the problem, information is required in sufficient detail to permit not only an awareness of its existence but an understanding of cause and effect. Thus, signals sent out by the control system must be capable of amplification and extension upon management's request.

Searching for alternative solutions requires information on the structure and processes involved in the particular problem area and on the interactions of this area with other parts of the organization. The linking of one alternative to others is greatly facilitated by proper structuring of the information system.

Evaluating the alternatives selected is closely linked with the search for the alternatives themselves but involves more detailed and explicit considerations of the effect of each alternative on the organization. It is at this stage that decision models and quantitative techniques play their most important role and where the demands for quantified planning data are greatest.

The selection of an alternative follows the evaluation process. If the problem can be specified in detail and if the evaluation model is both pertinent and complete, then the choice of an alternative logically follows from the evaluation. Often, however, one or more of these conditions is not fulfilled and selecting an alternative solution is far from automatic. It is in these cases that managerial judgment is applied and qualitative factors are merged with the quantitative results of the evaluation process.

Since the planning process revolves around the search for and the evaluation of alternatives, the information system should be designed to permit a variety of analyses including many whose characteristics are at present unknown. This requires the collection and processing of data in a relatively disaggregated form. The degree of disaggregation, in turn, depends upon the technical capabilities and the economic feasibilities of the information system.

To facilitate the planning process, information collected should reflect the major classes of alternatives that are most often evaluated. For example, if decisions are departmentalized, then the data could be centered around the alternatives of the foreman or the department or division manager. If the decision making is done on a product basis, the data should be collected to fit the decision-making scheme even if it cuts across departmental and functional lines.

The level of the planning activity provides additional guides. Overall goals and objectives must be established and alternatives evaluated at the top level of the organization. Plans must be made to achieve these goals and then, at a more detailed level, programs developed to implement these plans. Tasks are assigned to accomplish these programs and then actions are taken in performing these tasks. Each of these levels of decision requires information which, if not of a different type, is of different scope and level of detail. Further, the degree of structure of the planning process at each level conditions the information needed. The more highly programmed the activity, the greater the predictability of the information required and the consequent increase in the ability of the information system to provide the information needed as a matter of routine system design.

Finally, the types of decision models used in the planning process influence the data needed. Different methods of evaluating alternatives require different information in different forms. In addition, as the models become more sophisticated and as the evaluation process becomes more complete, the amount of quantitative information increases. This imposes additional requirements of a more explicit nature on the information system and substitutes, in some degree, quantitative information requirements at the evaluation stage for qualitative information at the selection stage.

Information for Control

Control deals almost exclusively with the conformance of actions to objectives, plans, or goals. Consequently, information for control focuses both on the actions taken and the selected plans and objectives they are supposed to achieve. This focus on planned accomplishments provides a framework for the collection of control data. Another framework is furnished by the organization through which the plans are implemented. Since both the plans and the mechanisms for implementing them are known, either before or as the actions proceed, the information utilized for control can be collected according to some predetermined structure—a situation that is in sharp contrast with planning information where the only structure available for governing the collection of information is the knowledge that alternative courses of action must be capable of evaluation. This contrast is heightened by the concern in planning with projected data while control involves reporting on what has occurred.

Control is not limited, however, merely to collecting information relating to the past. Of great importance is the comparison of what has happened with a standard of what should have occurred—the plan or objective. These plans and objectives are, to a significant degree, a matter of expectations and expectations vary continuously with time and with changing circumstances. Thus, what was set down as to what should occur may no longer be a rational basis for guiding or evaluating actions which are intended to achieve the organization's goals when the time comes for implementation. Consequently, management needs information not only on the changing actions of members of the organization but on the changing condition of the environment in which these actions take place.

As actions must be modified to accord to plans, so must the plans be modified to achieve the organization's goals. It is of particular importance that when evaluations of actions are made, the scope of judgment include the appropriateness of the standards or plans. The environmental conditions that now pertain are relevant to this judgment, not the conditions that were expected to be encountered.

The role of predetermined standards in controlling performance in an organization depends largely on the nature of the activities undertaken and on the environment in which they operate. Where the environmental conditions are determinable and where the activities may be programmed, predetermined standards play a large and useful role. Where the environment is uncertain or variable, but where the activities are programmed, predetermined standards can still be used and reports can be made comparing the actual against the expectations. This comparison, of course, is fundamental for control and is the basis of the principle of management by exception. With a variable environment, the exception directs management's attention not only to the appropriateness of the action but to that of the standard or expectation as well.

With unprogrammed activities, predetermined standards of performance and achievement are of less use. Less is known about the nature of the actions to be taken and the extent to which the goals, the actions, or the environment encountered influence the results. In these cases evaluations are often made on the results obtained rather than on the actions taken and are made against an ill-defined standard of what was considered possible to achieve—or perhaps what is considered a "satisfactory" level of accomplishment.

Control of unprogrammed activities, particularly within the time span between determinable results, often involves controlling effort rather than controlling results. Thus comparisons are made of what was spent relative to an expense budget rather than what was spent relative to what was accomplished. Here, as in other cases, the improvement of control lies in the development of better measures— which in turn depends upon increasing the level of knowledge of the processes under examination.

The control function is tied into planning through the feedback it provides on how well the plans have been conceived and implemented and in bringing to light problems that require managerial attention. To be effective, the information must be structured to reflect the activity or organizational unit under examination. Further, the information should reveal cause and effect relationships that exist so that the proper problems are highlighted while something can still be done about them.

In addition, the information should mirror the organization as it exists—highlighting the areas of managerial discretion and reflecting the integrated, overall plans governing the areas of programmed activity. As the organization or the planning process changes, so must the information structure adapt. Otherwise, managerial attention will be directed to the wrong areas and problems.

Information for control is usually expressed in quantitative terms and is concerned with the levels and rates of performance, amounts and value of resources used, and the quantities produced or other measures of task accomplishment. At the basic operating level, a great deal of control involves non-dollar data. At higher levels, where combinations of different activities are evaluated, dollar valuation is the rule. The accounting system is the major source of this latter information which contributes to the close identification of the accountant with the function of control.

A Summary of Information Needs

We have mentioned various phases of the planning and control functions of management. The interrelationships of these phases may be viewed as an endless loop as shown in the accompanying chart.

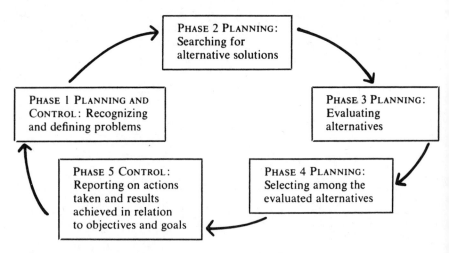

The accounting function has a particularly important role to play in the phases numbered 1, 3, and 5. Phase 1 provides the link between planning and control. It is the initial phase of the planning process and also the result, in part, of the control process. Phase 3, an important part of the planning process, is potentially a most productive area for management accounting. It requires imagination and resourcefulness as well as technical knowledge and environmental awareness. Phase 5 is the essence of the accountant's role in the control function. Accounting is less useful for Phases 2 and 4 in the planning process since these are less structured in nature and require a higher proportion of qualitative information.

The characteristics of control information for internal management and the information required for external reporting are similar in that they are both organized to reflect known, specified frameworks—such as departments or products for internal management, and financial condition and economic profitability (or resource expenditure in not-for-profit organizations) for external reporting. Planning information for internal management on the other hand is not amenable to such organization. Thus the planning needs of management provide the basic difference in design and structure of an information system intended for internal use and one intended solely for external reporting.

Finally, the characteristics of the control process, particularly the concern for what has been accomplished, have had considerable influence on accounting information. The complete and systematic manner in which accounting has responded to the requirements of organization control has caused the information it furnishes (for control purposes) to be widely used but at the same time severely criticized for being inappropriate to all the uses it has been put. Planning and decision making is one aspect of management and feedback and control the other. Information on what has occurred and what areas need investigation is useful for considering what succeeding actions should be, but it is not necessarily the best guide in the evaluation of possible alternatives. The particular role of accounting information in both these uses is discussed in some detail in the last section of this chapter.

APPLICATION OF ACCOUNTING STANDARDS

The standards for accounting information and the guidelines for communicating this information described in Chapter II apply equally to the general-purpose reports prepared for investors and others outside the firm and to the various studies and reports prepared for internal management use. While the same standards apply, there may be considerable variation in the degree of conformity with the various standards required for each particular management use. This section considers the applicability of the standards of accounting information— relevance, verifiability, freedom from bias, and quantifiability—and the guidelines for communication as they pertain to internal information. In addition, the major differences in the application of these standards between internal and external reporting are indicated.

Relevance

Relevance is at the heart of internal reporting. If information is not relevant to some need it is, indeed, worse than useless. Thus it is fortunate that the close relationship of the management accountant to all levels of informational use within the organization and his familiarity with the operations of the firm make it possible for him to determine relevance in a manner which more precisely reflects the needs, understanding, and receptivity of particular users. The sheer size and heterogeneity of the needs, levels of sophistication, and personal characteristics of users of externally reported data place serious limitations on the possibility of achieving any similar approach to relevance. This is not meant to imply that the demands placed upon the internal information system are any less heterogeneous or complex for, on the contrary, the number and variety of special reports prepared for internal use exceeds by orders of magnitude those destined for outside consumption.

The management accountant can and should rely on specification and feedback mechanisms that permit the needs of internal users to be communicated to the information system and the usefulness of the information to be ascertained by subsequent follow-up procedures. Thus, the information transmitted is dynamically monitored to ensure its relevance to the specified purpose.

This specification-feedback cycle characterizes the internal information function and permits it to focus on information designed for particular use. In contrast, external accounting reporting is accurately characterized by the term "general purpose financial reports," since the feedback mechanism is not so readily available.

A further difference between the communication of information within and without the organization lies in the extent to which detailed, disaggregated figures should be reported. Competitive pressures have exerted an influence on the accountant preparing reports for use outside the organization. He is required to balance the disclosure of relevant information with the need for concealment of "sensitive" details. Although a valid consideration, this rationale should not be abused. While still present, security is much less a factor in internal reporting and the lack of this restraint permits internal accounting to be of increased usefulness by providing both more in total and more highly purpose-related data to internal management.

Verifiability

Management users need assurance that accounting information possesses a suitable degree of verifiability. They also need to know of any major limitations or qualifications to the attainment of this standard. The degree of verifiability needed and the verification methods used may differ substantially in internal reporting from those applicable to information prepared for external use. The position of the independent certified public accountant in his external reporting role is different from that of the controller reporting to his management group. Indeed, the requirement of independent certification of the external reports is indicative of a greater need externally for verifiability.

Even within the organization, the degree of verifiability differs. Data obtained and information presented for evaluating alternative courses of action are less verifiable than those used for control. For control purposes, particularly the measurement of performance, an agreed upon, objectively-determinable measure of results is often of more use than a more "accurate" but subjective representation of the true state of affairs. For other aspects of control such as reporting on the extent to which plans are achieved, relevance may be weighted more heavily than verifiability when the two are in conflict. It is unfortunate that verifiability is difficult to achieve in the selection and evaluation of alternative courses of action. It is fortunate that it is not needed for planning to the same degree that it is in control.

Freedom from Bias

Deliberate insertion of personal bias into information prepared and communicated by accountants can rarely, if ever, be condoned. Bias in a statistical or measurement sense, however, may be acceptable. The accountant should go as far as possible to aid each manager he serves but he should remain cognizant of the information's potential use by others. Thus he should improve information content and means of presentation for each manager but not in a way that may prove detrimental to any other who may seek to utilize this same information.

This does not mean, however, that statistically biased information should not be used. Particularly in dealing with planning information, a measurement technique that produces a consistent estimation that comes closer to the actual value, but with a known deviation, can often be more useful than estimates that average out to the true value, but have wider error ranges. Provided the necessary qualifications are noted, including the degree and direction of any statistical bias, there need be no logical objection to its use in internal accounting.

Control information within the firm can also contain bias where the bias is known and of an impersonal nature. Branch offices may be charged "costs" which in fact contain an element of profit or products may be valued at cost based on a standard that does not represent "full, economic costs." While no doubt useful, biased measures create a problem. For over time, these figures may be used for purposes for which they are not relevant without adjustment for the bias and the presence of this bias is either forgotten or ignored. An example is the use of LIFO-based inventory. Here, the direction and methodology, if not the exact amount of the bias, are known, yet the balance sheet figure is used in inappropriate calculations such as the current financial ratio.

Another widely used instrument for management control is the budget. In budgeting, sales volume figures may be used that are based on optimistic estimates that are more in the nature of goals than expectations. When used as a goal this bias may be appropriate but when used for planning it is far less useful. It is hoped that recognition of the function of accounting to serve the many aspects of management involved in planning and control will heighten the sensitivity to bias and help to eliminate this problem. In addition, as more and more of the internal information, such as budgets, become a part of external reports, the need for elimination of such biased figures is required.

Quantifiability

The need for quantified data in external reporting is unquestioned. Yet the form and type of measures used must be clear and understandable. This factor limits the form of the information provided external users but should be viewed as a constraint that will be less and less a factor as owners and investors increase in sophistication.

For internal use, however, the types of measures used and the form of the information presented is limited only by the capabilities of the accountant and the sophistication of a far fewer number of people. Thus accounting information may be communicated internally, for example, as a single number (a point estimate), as an interval estimate, a probability distribution, or by other means provided the recipient of the information is prepared to deal with the particular formulation.

The management accountant reporting to the external world can rarely be as informed of the capabilities or even the needs of his audience.

Particularly for planning purposes, accounting information could usefully be expressed in probabilistic terms since the estimates of the consequences of the various alternatives being evaluated are held with uncertainty—less certainty, surely, than the results of actions that have taken place. The communication of the nature and degree of the uncertainty is an important part of the evaluation and accounting should not shy away from facing this responsibility.

The factor of quantifiability was used in relating the accountant's information more closely to the evaluation of already selected alternatives than to the process of selecting the best one. The standard of quantification is no less important within the firm than without. Indeed, the range of methods available to meet this standard poses one of the most significant challenges to the discipline of accounting.

Guidelines for Communication

Issues related to the guidelines for communication have been raised in discussing accounting information. The separation of the requirements placed upon accounting information as between planning and control has been dictated by its appropriateness to the expected use. Disclosure of significant relationships has been touched upon in the problem of aggregation and is directly confronted in the recognition that the design of the information system must reflect the system that exists if managerial evaluations and subsequent decisions are to be meaningful. Disclosure of significant relationships is also the governing consideration in the provision of information for the evaluation of alternatives.

Inclusion of environmental information is particularly relevant where information for both planning and for control is prepared. The data collected and the information prepared in the evaluation of an alternative course of action may not be appropriate for control purposes or for further evaluations once the alternative is selected and becomes a reality. Similarly, the information collected for controlling an ongoing activity is seldom, if ever, useful for evaluating the activity against other alternatives. The purpose for which the information is prepared and the implicit assumptions which this preparation entails are a necessary part of the figures.

Uniformity of practice and consistency through time apply particularly to information of a scorekeeping nature prepared as part of managerial control. Without consistency, the effect of alterations in plans over time would be difficult to detect and evaluate. Without uniformity of practice, various alternative operations could not be properly evaluated nor could performance be rewarded in some cases and corrective actions taken in others.

The uses of management information have been examined and the standards governing accounting information have been applied. It is necessary to extend the analysis and examine the accounting system to indicate the mechanisms by which the needed accounting information can be provided.

FULFILLING MANAGEMENT'S INFORMATION NEEDS

The conventional view of an accounting system considers past data as the basic input, the chart of accounts as the basic classification model, and the financial statements as the basic output. This concept, when supplemented by current valuations, is a reasonably adequate basis for the general purpose statements discussed in Chapter III. It also provides management with information that is relevant to the planning and control of its activities through the aggregation and classification of the same basic data by the different functions and decision levels within the organization. This internal function is accomplished by preparing in varying detail financial reports (a) for contemplated alternatives, (b) on the performance of cost or profit centers, or (c) for the operations of the various product groups that exist within the organization. Useful as it is, the committee believes that a concept of accounting restricted to such a system is too narrow a view of what accounting is today and much too narrow a framework from which to view the potential of management accounting in future years.

Examining the needs of management for quantitative information reveals both the importance of the information produced through the conventional accounting system and the necessity for expanding this concept to include information that meets the standards of accounting but which is often viewed as falling outside of the conventional model described above. Recognizing this situation, the committee has separated its examination of management's needs for accounting information into two categories: Accounting Information from the Conventional Model and Accounting Information Provided Separately from the Conventional Model.[4] This has been done solely for expository purposes and should not be taken to mean that the committee views the accounting function as being so dichotomized. Quite the contrary is in

---

4. By conventional model we mean the framework that is used for producing general-purpose, externally-oriented accounting statements and reports.

fact true. The committee believes that a unified accounting function which encompasses both categories of information is not only desirable but necessary if the accounting function is to be effectively performed.

Accounting Information from the Conventional Model

The oldest and perhaps the most basic part of an "accounting system" is the portion that involves recording the impact on the organization of economic phenomena and recognizing the effects of transactions as they occur. This function is based on operational principles stemming from economic theory. Consequently, the product of the basic accounting system is a measure of the position and the operations of the organization in economic terms. Since the operations of almost all organizations involve economic considerations—with profit maximation being a major goal of most—the output from this accounting system provides possibly the most useful framework for evaluating an organization's activities and assessing its accomplishments.

The information that is used to evaluate the past is also useful in planning for the future. Examination of the past, particularly with multiperiod evaluation of trends, is one of the best methods for forecasting future conditions and, hence, for guiding management's activities. The accounting model provides a format for projecting and evaluating results of contemplated and diverse alternatives and serves as a means of common expression (in the form of investment, profit, and rate of return) of the projected outcome of the complex factors that bear on the firm's operations.

The processes of setting long-term and short-term goals of the firm, the corresponding long- and short-term sub-goals of organizational units within the firm, and the testing of these goals for feasibility and internal consistency all utilize the accounting model. From a traditional point of view, accounting is considered to serve the planning function best when goals and sub-goals can be expressed in terms of income and its contributing factors, but it is also useful if goals can be expressed in terms of financial concepts such as assets, creditor and owner claims, costs to achieve, profitability, and solvency. As noted later, the accounting model does not always serve best as an expression of the degree of success resulting from specific management actions. It does, however, indicate results relative to an overall profit goal.

The expression of sub-unit results in terms of an overall profit framework raises the problem that the measured result becomes an end in itself and that some decisions may be made in anticipation of the way in which the results will be reported rather than the way in which the underlying objectives are achieved. This is of concern only where the measure does not correspond to the goal but is of importance when methods applicable to measuring the results of economic entities are applied to interdependent units within the firm. Here, overall goals may suffer when the sub-unit attempts to maximize its reported profit by, say, engaging in activities that worsen the performance of another unit— for example, omitting maintenance of a commonly used facility.

One of the most practical means of improving the ability of the conventional accounting model to evaluate alternatives is to provide classifications which reflect cause and effect relationships. Therefore, many costs should be classified into fixed, variable, and variants of these categories with known measures of the magnitude of their responses to causal factors to which they are most meaningfully related. The dynamic nature of most enterprises requires frequent review of such determinations and adjustments to recognize changing circumstances.

The development of general budgets involves projections prepared typically by many individuals within a firm. This process is made easier and accuracy is increased if the "accounting system" has developed historical data in capsules which correspond to the capsules that individuals must contribute to the budget. This is the planning aspect of "responsibility accounting" which has control as its most obvious purpose.

The effectiveness of the conventional accounting system for producing data for management control has already been discussed. This function is facilitated if the collection and presentation of the information is done by areas of managerial responsibility and discretion. Responsibility arrangement of data and the integration within the accounting model of standards and budgets have, in fact, become basic for most firms. The role of accounting systems in creating cost consciousness and in providing a basis for evaluation and reward is well known. In addition, its measurements provide the basis for the principle of management by exception. Profit and investment centers are a vivid illustration of the use of accounting for control in the latter term's broadest sense. The disciplines of the balance sheet, the income statement, and the comparison of budgeted with actual performance represent the most effective single set of controls used by management to date.

The conventional accounting model, through the correspondence of its output with the profit objective and the determination of financial position, serves the function of overall management control quite well. By examining its output over time, forecasts of the future can be made.

For controlling individual sub-units wtihin the organization, the conventional model is also effective but not without some limitations when operating on a disaggregated level. Finally, it provides a framework for planning resource allocations and for budgeting and coordinating diverse activities. In planning, particularly in the evaluation of alternative courses of action, the conventional accounting model lacks applicability. It is predominantly in this direction that the committee's recommendations for extension are found.

Accounting Information Provided Separately from the Conventional Model

The management role of accounting should not be restricted to recombining, summarizing, and projecting the data gathered for the owners, the enterprise, or the government. Indeed, a number of other uses have developed around the conventional accounting model which utilize its results in a modified or special form. In addition, internal accounting personnel are active in preparing information for special studies and in gathering data that are outside the conventional structure.

Recognizing that accounting will continue to develop in scope and importance, the committee proposes that the collection and processing of economic data which meet the standards set forth in this study be recognized as an essential part of accounting, and that the output of these processes, whether projected or historical in nature, whether single-valued or in probabilistic form, and whether expressed in monetary units or other terms, be considered as results of the accounting function.

In addition to the developments in the theory of management which provide increased structure for evaluating the information needed by internal management, two additional factors are changing the nature of the internal accounting function. First, the evaluation of alternative courses of action increasingly involves analytic tools which can deal more effectively with the multidimensional aspects that are pertinent to managerial problems and which can utilize data simultaneously in a variety of forms (such as dollar costs, rates of flow, and capacity restrictions). Second, electronic computers can quickly and economically collect and process data from a variety of sources to serve a multiplicity of ends. These factors are tending to blur the distinctions, at least operationally, between accounting and non-accounting information and to alter the information functions performed. The problem of the accounting theorist is to evaluate the impact of developments in the management sciences and in computer technology on (1) the consistency of his model, (2) its scope, and (3) the assumptions upon which it is based. The problem of the accounting practitioner is to meet the expanding challenge for relevant information.

In meeting the requirements of management for relevant information, the accountant should go beyond historically-valued transaction data. Particularly in evaluating alternatives, traditional accounting information is inadequate and is being supplemented by data outside of the traditional model. As demands for information specific to particular decision models have increased, the accountant has become involved both in data and in analytic techniques, for the one cannot be used (obtained) without some knowledge of the other. Increased attention is being given to the analytic and behavioral underpinnings of the accounting discipline itself. Accountants should be alert to recognize the many new functions they must perform and the changing nature of their role in business management.

The remainder of this chapter illustrates the changing characteristics of management information for both planning and control. Speculation on the directions which accounting will take in the future is presented in Chapter V.

Planning: Marginal analysis has been a tool of the economist in explaining and understanding the behavior of economic units for many years, but only within the last few decades have these techniques been applied and the measuring apparatus developed to permit widespread use in making rational decisions within the firm. Conventional break-even techniques with all of their variations provide an illustration. Profit sensitivity analysis has become a basic tool in the performance of the planning function. Marginal costs and revenues have become crucial to decisions involving pricing policy, product line emphasis, and production volume levels.

A part of marginal analysis technique involves cost behavior studies and attempts to implement knowledge of cost and revenue responses to various causal factors. This effort has led to an emphasis upon concepts of incremental and decremental costs, revenues, and profits. While most of the work in this area has been limited to models that consider only linear relationships with a single variable, developments in mathematical programming permit the consideration of non-linear patterns with many variables simultaneously.

Another set of analytical practices which is rapidly becoming an accepted management tool relates to the use of time-adjusted cash flow projections in justifying capital expenditures. Several methods of combining basic data are in current use. These include some that explicitly deal with risk considerations and can incorporate such considerations as the payback period as constraints. These methods involve recourse to analytic models in combination with computer techniques. Although the methodology of marginal analysis is not seen as fitting naturally into the conventional accounting model, it is an important tool of management accounting and is becoming incorporated therein— even to the extent of making its influence felt in external reporting.

The development and manipulation of models for inventory policy and control provides another example of analytical techniques separate from the conventional "system." The management accountant plays an important role in providing the data these models depend upon and in appraising their applicability in determining economic order quantities, minimum inventory levels, and general policy with regard to inventory planning. In addition, these models are being linked with financial considerations and even into the conventional accounting budget system.

Finally, there is the technique of simulation, which, by itself or in conjunction with one or more analytic models, is proving to be one of the more useful techniques in dealing with complex business problems. Utilizing the capabilities of large, high-speed computers, complex problems for which analytic techniques are inadequate may be investigated by means of iterative procedures using either Monte-Carlo (probabilistic or random draws) or heuristic (rules of thumb search procedures) techniques. Such techniques have been utilized in a number of problem areas including cash flow projections, capital budgeting, securities portfolio management, and in production and marketing decisions.

Control: Although the conventional accounting model serves the financial control function of management reasonably well, new developments in technology are altering the organizational structure with consequent effects upon the control process and the information it requires. Two directions appear in evidence at the present time. The first is that control will increasingly be exerted across functional lines to mirror the integrated organization brought about by the computer. The second direction is the type and level of control which will become a much less personal-contact-oriented function and one which relies heavily upon technical knowledge and programs of "automatic control." In fact, budgets for evaluation are today being prepared after the fact based on optimization models of what should have been. It is but a short step for these to go "on-line" and to monitor performance in real-time. There is no question but that accounting information will continue to be involved in these and the other mentioned developments. The major problem is that of providing an orderly growth toward the future without losing the value of established practices and the lessons of the past.

CHAPTER V

EXTENSION OF ACCOUNTING THEORY

Because of technological changes and advances in knowledge of human behavior the scope and methods of accounting are changing and can be expected to continue to change. This chapter takes note of some of the patterns emerging and suggests areas for future accounting research as well as a possible outline of the dimensions of accounting theory of the future.

Major areas in which changes are occurring which will influence accounting in the future are perceived as including:

1. Knowledge of decision processes.

2. Knowledge of human behavior.

3. Computer technology and systems design.

4. Measurement techniques and information theory.

In the light of these developments accounting theory and practice will probably be broadened considerably in the future. A possible structure of future accounting theory will be more normative and less descriptive than in the past. The scope of accounting may include the measurement and communication of data revealing past, present, and prospective socio-economic activities. Improvement of control methods and decision making at all levels will become major goals of accounting.

Accounting may well merge with other separate disciplines with the result that a new "information profession" will evolve. For this transition to occur and for the accountant to maintain his present relative position calls for added research into the following areas:

1. Information needs of individuals and organizations both in terms of what is and what should be. Such needs must be discovered and analyzed if the services rendered by information reporting are to be improved.

2. Impact of measurements on human actions.

3. Improvement of measurement and communication techniques.

Until much more is learned about each of these areas, the boundaries and structure of accounting theory of the future must remain somewhat indeterminate.

Prefatory Note

The committee believes that there are many areas in accounting that warrant intensive research. It hopes to encourage this type of research by including, as the last chapter of this statement on basic accounting theory, a discussion of the possible nature and scope of future accounting theory.

Conceptual Bases of Accounting

Essentially, accounting is an information system. More precisely, it is an application of a general theory of information to the problem of efficient economic operations. It also makes up a large part of the general information systems which provide decision-making information expressed in quantitative terms. In this context accounting is both a part of the general information system of an operating entity and a part of a basic field bounded by the concept of information.

Accounting is also concerned with effective transmission or communication of information. The committee believes the accounting communication method is in need of re-examination. The assumptions of the preparers of the statements and the reactions of the recipients of the information need to be explored. The problem may lend itself to systematic research, for recent developments in the behavioral sciences suggest that the reactions and needs of the people preparing and using reports are capable of study. This suggests that the study of accounting in the future may well include research on the behavioral aspects of accounting information.

Accounting is a measurement process which may be applied to a variety of activities. It is also a distinctive applied information system which provides information for economic decisions. It is distinctive in that, among other characteristics, the results it produces must meet the standards of relevance, verifiability, freedom from bias, and quantifiability. In this sense, accounting is one of the applied quantitative fields in the complex encompassed by the notion of measurement theory.

Scope of Future Accounting

Accounting may be distinguished from other applied information systems by the methods it uses and the activities it measures. Historically, the methods of the accounting discipline have largely been confined to the double-entry bookkeeping mechanism, the discipline of arithmetic, and certain conventional measurement tools. The activities with which accounting has been concerned have been those transactions involving financial data. It is, of course, evident that the accounting discipline could be expanded, either by absorbing additional measurement methods into the discipline or by broadening the concept of activities upon which it reports.

Recent developments in measurement methods coupled with the advent of the computer indicate a significant increase in the ability of accounting to develop information. Increased complexity and size of organizations in society suggest a demand for more information as does the development of explicit, analytic decision models. Thus the pressures exist for an expansion of the scope of accounting. The committee believes that initially this expansion will be reflected in accounting reports with multiple valuations. Multi-dimensional reporting may also be expected to increase. One aspect of multiple valuations is reflected in the simultaneous use of several measurements such as historical acquisition costs, estimates of purchasing power equivalents using general price-level adjustments, current costs, and current values. The committee has taken a first step by recommending two-column reports emphasizing historical cost and current cost. Another aspect of multiple valuations involves the use of non-deterministic measures or quantum ranges[1] with or without probabilistic[2] measures. In view of uncertainties surrounding business activities and the measurement of their impact, the use of such non-deterministic measures is likely to become a part of an expanded accounting discipline of the future.

The multi-dimensional aspects of accounting involve measurement against more than one goal or objective, where each possesses its own unit of measurement. While the measurement process currently focuses on economic dollar-valued data and relates the performance of the organization to either profitability or to the extent of budgeted expenditure, accounting in the future can well consider several aspects of a transaction or event simultaneously. For example, a sale may involve the following three measures, (1) a measure of revenues and costs in dollars—related to the profit objective; (2) a measure of employee or consumer satisfaction in its own terms—related to future productivity or market potential; and (3) a measure of, say, the national interest involved in the sale—the amount of which has to be maintained at some minimal level by government decree. These would be aggregated separately over all transactions and the results compared to the three separate and basically incommensurable objectives.

Nature of Future Accounting Information

Within the bounds of future accounting, the standards of relevance, verifiability, freedom from bias, and quantifiability may take on more precise meanings. The notion that accounting information must be relevant to the action or decision under consideration is a relative concept, and new measurement methods may enable an improvement in the degree of relevance of accounting information. Should such an

---

1. For example "inventory is estimated at $1,040,800 ± $200,000."

2. To extend the example of footnote 1 "the inventory is estimated at $1,040,800 ± $200,000 on a 95% confidence basis."

improvement occur, information now supported in theory as appropriate or relevant because no better information is available may be considered theoretically inappropriate in the future.

In addition, user needs may change in the future. In fact, it has been widely proclaimed in management literature that the income motive alone is no longer the objective of many large business entities. If accounting is to provide relevant information in an economy motivated by multiple objectives, accounting theory in the future may treat information now considered irrelevant to both internal and external users as relevant.

The possibility exists that in the future information will be so complete in many areas that decision making in the traditional sense will not exist. In an automated factory, for example, many decisions formerly made by people are even now made by machines on the basis of information automatically collected. This development represents a merger of the information function and the decision function. Where it occurs, some previous decisions of management follow automatically from the accounting information. This development can take place, however, only if the information meets the verifiability standard.

To comply with the standard of verifiability, accounting data must necessarily be supported by somewhat standardized evidence. This means that verifiability could be created by establishing standardized ways of measuring activities. The implication of this situation is that accounting theory of the future may deal with methods of making data more verifiable than it has in the past because of the growing importance of information in economic society.

The notion of evidence may take on more of a relative meaning in the future. For example, the absolutely verifiable evidence of the market price of a piece of land may be the price at which it is sold. It is possible, however, by proper sampling of land prices, to determine an estimated market price before the land is sold. Such an estimated market price would be more verifiable than the opinion of one person regarding the market price of the land. In fact, the relatively less verifiable market price established by sampling may come to be very useful accounting data even though the least verifiable market price established by the personal opinion of one man would not. This opens for discussion the degree of probability needed before phenomena may be accepted as evidence and the implication is that accounting research might well be directed to the task of developing and establishing verifiable data.

EXTENSION OF ACCOUNTING THEORY

To an increasing extent, accounting literature implies a need for the theoretical aspects of accounting to be less of an explanation or a rationalization of practice than it often has been. Departure from mere explanation or rationalization of the applied field would cause accounting theory to turn to another type of freedom from bias: a freedom from uncertainty regarding the reasoning process in deductively establishing theoretical statements. This possibility is based on the assumption that the more abstract part of future accounting theory may be closely tied to scientific methods.

Current accounting literature now refers to measurement methods not considered in past statements of accounting theory. This development of accounting theory as a type of measurement theory raises the issue of the relationship of future accounting theory to statistics, economics, and a host of social science fields concerned with measurement theory. It may happen, of course, that the measurement aspects of all these separate divisions may merge into one overall measurement discipline at the theory level and that the applied counterpart would be "The Information Profession." But it seems more realistic to assume that the separate areas will exist but that the overlapping portions at the fringes will expand. Such a development is sufficiently likely for the committee to suggest that accounting research might well be extended in the direction of measurement theory. The committee proposes that accounting theory should be expanded in the future so as to deal with accounting practice as the operation of an information system. This means that future theory constructions should deal with the nature and validity of various measurement methods which should be used in accounting.

The Future Accounting Information System

An overview of the anticipated issues of future accounting theory carries implications regarding the future accounting information system. That is, one conception of a future accounting system could include as accounting inputs all quantitative data gathered for whatever purposes and as accounting outputs all internal reports for planning, directing and controlling purposes, as well as the basic public statements. Thus the future accounting information system could include projected information that fits into the conventional classification model and also all non-transaction data, whether past or projected, whether collected from sources internal or external to the firm, that may be useful for the direction of entity activities.

Integration of all data collection, storage and synthesis, and communication functions within the firm is a natural and desirable objective. It is now approaching a realizable state particularly because of advances taking place in the utilization of large-scale computers. Integration of applied information systems has the advantage of centralizing authority for the development and maintenance of the system, eliminating gaps and duplication in the data processing function, and improving accuracy, consistency, and control of information. Thus, one important objective in the design of future accounting systems is to integrate as far as possible the wide variety of data sources and data uses in order to deal with the multiple characteristics and ramifications of every activity. The development of such a future accounting information system will be a most involved process. Research on system design and development should be tied back to such fields as systems enginering and information theory.

Outline of a Possible Structure of the Future Accounting Theory

The preceding discussion of the nature of future accounting data and actions is based on the assumption that accounting theory of the future will be more normative and less descriptive than it has in the past. The committee concludes that the assumption is valid and that future accounting theory should place emphasis on the normative aspects of accounting measurements and communication.

The nature of future accounting can be seen only in dim outline and it is premature to suggest a detailed framework for a theoretical structure of future accounting. But it may be appropriate to suggest a general outline of such a structure in order to direct attention to the need for broad theoretical studies of the accounting discipline. Such an outline may be developed under three headings as follows:

I. Scope of the Discipline

    A. Objective of the accounting function: Measurement and communication of data revealing past, present, and prospective socio-economic activities.

    B. Underlying disciplines used in performing the accounting function: Behavioral sciences, mathematics, and such less well-defined areas as information theory and computer science, as well as the conventional accounting methods.

    C. Purpose of the accounting function: To improve control methods and decision making at all levels of socio-economic activities.

II. Nature of Accounting Concepts
  A. Motivation concepts: The cause of socio-economic activities
     must be related to individual wants and organizational goals
     such as the desire for income (short- and long-term), prestige,
     power, and mixed and conflicting objectives.

  B. Measurement concepts: The assumptions made to facilitate
     the measurement process such as those bearing on the nature
     of an accounting entity, a determination of the activities to
     be measured, and the selection of an appropriate measure-
     ment unit.

  C. Communication concepts: The assumptions made to facilitate
     the transmission of information involving such issues as the
     selection of the measurement language used, the determina-
     tion of effective reporting methods, and the direction of in-
     formation to its best use.

III. Elements of the Discipline
  A. Accounting methods: This includes such techniques as the
     computer, statistical analyses, and a variety of other measure-
     ment methods.

  B. Accounting entities: This includes any organizational unit
     such as business units, governmental agencies, nations or
     regions, and individuals.

  C. Accounting activities: These represent selected points in the
     flow of socio-economic activities such as transactions and
     other objective points in the flow process.

From such a conception of the proper outline of future accounting
theory, it is possible to suggest a variety of areas of basic research which
might be undertaken to contribute to the development of such a structure. A list of such areas would include, among others, the following:

  1. The nature of social, organizational, and individual wants. The
     greatest accounting need both at present and in the future is the
     determination of the nature of the information needs of users of
     accounting communications. No one really knows what individ-
     uals or any organization wants, or what they should want, and
     there is a need for some fundamental research on this question.
     There may be ethical aspects to this issue for the instinctive wants
     of individuals may not be the wants most needed for society.
     But, more important, there is a need for research on organiza-
     tional goals in relation to the goals of individuals. It is generally

recognized that there is a hierarchy of social and individual values and this means that it is not enough to know what organizational wants are. It is also necessary to know the relative importance of each want under different conditions. Research in this area apparently would be directed to a determination of the causes of individual and organizational wants. The results should throw light on accounting needs under different conditions and in pursuit of different goals. Research here should also involve investigating the interrelations of the decision models of the users with the nature and form of the information required and of the accounting model itself. Not only can information influence the decision process but the decision process influences the information required. Further, the nature of the theoretical structure of accounting is closely linked with certain of these models (network theory) and developments in one influence our understanding of the other.

2. The impact of measurements on human actions. Man appears to be influenced by the type of information he is given and there is a great need to know how different accounting measurements will influence the thinking of decision-makers and society in general. The possibility exists that measurements supplied to individuals will ultimately influence their thinking to such an extent that social and economic activities may be redirected by different measurement methods. For example, if an individual is judged as successful or unsuccessful in terms of some objective measurement, it is not unrealistic to assume that the individual will learn to perform so as to maximize his success indicator measurement. In so doing the individual may not be motivated to make socially desirable changes in his activities until the method by which his success indicator is measured is changed. This issue needs to be studied and related to accounting measurements.

3. The nature of information and measurement. Recent developments in social science measurement methods suggest a need for a reexamination of accounting measurements. Measurement is so closely allied to information that improvements in measurements will increase information. Since information reduces uncertainty, the nature of information must be investigated in terms of the nature of uncertainty. Coupling these considerations with others in the area of human communications suggests a need to provide a bridge between current accounting theory and the new

developments. One starting point would be an empirical study of all information flows within a firm. Such a study would disclose the extensive amount of information now transmitted outside the scope of the present accounting information system and it would disclose the measurement problem involved in quantifying certain information in order to fit it into a future accounting information system.

Until considerably more research of this type provides more information, it is premature to suggest any particularization of the theoretical structure of future accounting.

MEANS OF OBTAINING CURRENT-COST DATA

Chapter III contains a recommendation for the making and reporting of multiple measurements of economic and financial data to increase their utility to external users. A case was built, on the grounds of relevance, for the communication of a current expression in the form of replacement cost of the economic significance of the resources acquired, utilized, and held by an accounting entity. Here we consider the question of whether certain approaches to the quantification of replacement cost produce information which meets the standards of verifiability and freedom from bias.

Attention is directed primarily to those resources for which measurements of current cost are more likely to be the subject of controversy. It should be understood that the principle of reporting in current terms can be applied to all resources, obligations, and equities found in an accounting entity.

The scope of the discussion is also limited because certain items such as cash on hand and in banks are always reported in current terms and because some items are immaterial, such as supplies and other current prepaid items. In yet other instances, discussion is restricted simply because current practice seeks a measurement which is also a current expression of the economic significance of the items involved; this is true for accounts and notes receivable and for a variety of short-term liabilities.[1] The controversial areas include inventories and the various types of long-lived assets, both tangible and intangible.

Inventories

Accounting practice has long sanctioned references to current market value (either purchase price or reproduction cost) in seeking monetary measurements of inventories. While such references have generally been used as a basis for reporting only downward revisions of recorded amounts, it is significant that accountants have long been willing to recognize increases in the value of inventories where the increases are routinely verifiable. Some cases in point are basic commodities traded on organized exchanges and gold. Such commodities

---

1. Leaving aside the possible recognition of implicit interest in the valuation of current assets and liabilities as immaterial.

as wheat and other grains, cotton, some meat products and, in some localities, basic metals, fall in this category. In these industries not only are increases in the value of physical inventories recorded but accrued gains on purely executory contracts—futures contracts—are recorded and reported. Because of its fixed price and assured market, at least in the United States, gold is customarily recorded at its selling price less cost of disposal. In all of these cases the evidence of current market value is clear from the pervasive character of the quoted price and from the absence of a sales promotion problem. Frequent fluctuations in market price do not prevent the recording of adjustments to current value; only in the face of evidence of really extreme circumstances will a closing price be ignored—as, for example, when it is proved to be due to a crop reporting error that is corrected shortly after the date in question.

In the process of approving reductions to market in applying the "cost-or-market" rule, accountants have developed techniques for determining market values to be compared with cost. The current replacement cost of merchandise inventories can usually be secured from the supplier's current catalogue. Consideration, of course, must be given to freight and other in-transit costs as well as to cash and quantity discounts, if any. In manufacturing situations, market is deemed to be replacement cost based upon current prices for materials and labor and customary overhead costs. An upward limit to such measures of replacement cost is selling price less costs of completion and disposition.

The committee concludes that techniques presently used to determine current replacement cost produce information which is sufficiently verifiable, quantifiable, and free from bias to justify their use in stating inventories of merchandise, materials, and supplies at their current replacement cost. The bias inherent in the cost-or-market rule is replaced with the consistent application of an unbiased replacement-cost measurement. No problem of quantification appears to be involved which has not been solved in traditional practice.

Long-Term Investments

Blocks of stock large enough to establish a subsidiary or significant affiliated company relationship may have a market price per share different from that determined through an exchange of a smaller number of shares on an organized exchange. But these possible values per share are usually not verifiable in the absence of a valid contract to sell. They are also lacking in freedom from bias in many instances and so do not meet the standards established for accounting information. Quoted market prices are verifiable and free from bias and thus may be used although there may be some question as to whether they meet fully the standard of relevance. If no market values are available, a current cost may be obtained by computing book value after current cost measurements have been compiled for the issuing company in the manner suggested here for enterprises in general.

Relatively small blocks of stock, bonds, and mortgage notes of other concerns or persons are most accurately reflected on a current basis by market quotations whenever they are traded specifically. For mortgage notes, which are unique in certain respects, market quotations for similar classes or types are often available to establish a market value. For relatively small blocks of securities not regularly traded, a general price-level adjustment will constitute a minimum adjustment.

Equipment and Machinery

Among the approaches to the ascertainment of the current replacement cost of equipment and machinery are the following:

(1) Purchase price, new, on the current market, adjusted for depreciation. Where the same equipment or machinery, or a service equivalent, is available on a continuing basis, the catalogue price, adjusted as required for trade discounts, freight and otherwise, is a clear indication of current replacement cost. It is to be emphasized that service equivalents form the basis for determining replacement cost; replacement in kind is not the criterion.

(2) Purchase price, used, in the current market. Such a market may exist for only a limited number of types of equipment and machinery. When it does, current replacement cost can be determined by ascertaining the acquisition price of items similar to those held. It is to be noted that this is suggested as a basis for recognizing specific environmental changes and not as a basis for calculating depreciation where there is no evidence of environmental change.

(3) In those cases where new equipment or machinery is available only in more efficient form, so that a new machine of the same capacity does the work at less operating cost, downward adjustment (considering the relative capacity and costs of operation) to reflect this obsolescence in calculating current cost of the old equipment would be appropriate.

(4) Adjustment to current cost can be approximated through use of a specific price-level index for equipment of the broad classification

within which the equipment falls. In cases where the equipment or machinery is unique and not available from a continuing source of supply, this is evidently the only usable technique. In any case when an upward adjustment is indicated, care must be exercised to state the equipment at an amount no higher than can be recovered from the revenue generated through its use.

We conclude that the foregoing techniques will produce quantified current-cost information for equipment and machinery which is verifiable and free from bias.

Buildings

Few buildings are reproduced in a form faithful to the original design, building method, or materials; progress in the building arts exists to a striking degree. This fact is often cited to support the contention that any current cost calculated for buildings will not meet the tests of verifiability and freedom from personal bias. But, while buildings differ, their uses may be classifiable; office buildings are not confused with warehouses, warehouses are not confused with hotels, and so on. Where a building actually has more than one potential use, it may be identified with the class of use to which it is currently devoted. Furthermore, types of construction are classifiable and are the subject of much attention in the engineering and construction literature. To some extent such classifications form a basis for property tax assessments.

A substantial volume of price-index data is also continually accumulated on the construction industry, and popular newspaper reports on expected rates of overall construction costs are frequently quoted in connection with construction industry wage negotiations and settlements. These statistics are not prepared by accountants as a group; they are the product of specialists in the construction trades, particularly civil engineers, and they are to some degree prepared by government agencies. We suggest that such indices of building replacement costs are sufficiently well designed to provide quantifiable data which qualify as valid information; that they avoid personal bias on the part of managers and any significant statistical bias; and in view of their continual publication they are more than sufficiently verifiable from the accountant's viewpoint. We recommend that building replacement-cost indices for service equivalents be used as a primary basis for determining current costs for buildings.

Use of service equivalents is necessary due to a changing technology. The present cost to construct 100,000 square feet of warehouse space that will last for 30 years is a satisfactory current-cost approximation, with proper regard for depreciation, for a building originally built to provide the same space for the same length of time even though the materials and construction methods differ somewhat.

A question is likely to arise with regard to special local conditions— the building that commands a high rental value because of short local supply, or the building that is usable at only half-capacity because of low local demand. The latter problem exists without regard to current cost and should be recognized, as it often is, either in traditional depreciation policy or by a write-down or both. The question of high local value we feel is a reflection of land values, not building values, and we consider it below.

We conclude on this point that verifiable data, free from bias, in properly quantified form are actually or potentially available to make possible the ascertainment of current costs for buildings on a replacement cost-index basis. It should be noted in this regard that a widespread demand for such data for general accounting usage would further stimulate their production and perhaps also increase their reliability.

Land

Land is a unique asset. Each piece, strictly speaking, is to some degree unlike any other. But this point of view is easily overemphasized. For any ordinary purpose one downtown office building lot may serve as well as another nearby lot. Land values are the subject of constant transactions and continual reporting; in many jurisdictions the price of a real estate transaction must be a matter of public record for tax or other reasons. In many cases the price of land and of the improvements, including buildings, is one amount with no explicit reference to the relative values for each. In these circumstances, there may be sales of unimproved but otherwise closely comparable property to permit a realistic current costing of the land, and in some cases value of the land may be determined by deducting the replacement cost of improvements from the total price. Where no reasonably comparable recent sales are recorded, we recommend as a minimum that land be valued at historical cost adjusted by an index of land values for the area, preferably by an index for land put to similar use. Such indices, where prepared by independent, responsible agencies not directly concerned with the accountant's problems are, once again, verifiable, free of significant bias, and relevant to the user's needs.

Mineral and Other Natural Resources

In general, the determination of current costs for these assets parallels the techniques outlined for land used as building sites, but probably presents an easier problem. Data are available on the prices at which mineral deposits and rights and other natural resources are sold. A special problem here is the estimate of the amount of the resource involved. Managers in industries exploiting natural resources secure such data from engineering and geological estimates. For example, standing timber is purchased and sold on the basis of engineering surveys, and periodically checked by similar means. Rates of growth are measured by foresters. The data prepared by qualified practitioners in these fields may be used to determine the current cost of standing timber, including its accretion through growth, especially when the work is done by independent professionals. Accountants should use the estimates of reputable professional engineers or geologists as a basis for calculating the quantity of a resource just as others rely on accounting reports for relevant, quantified information.

No new problem is raised by the discovery of a mineral resource; explorations to determine quantity and quality are needed by management to plan exploitation, and the usual references to current costs of acquisition of similar salable material adjusted for transportation and separation costs provide a current-cost basis for the deposit. In cases of discovery and measurement solely by the employees of the owner, the independent public accountant, who states his opinion on the financial statements of the owner, may wish to have an independent geologist's opinion as to the contents of the ore body. The accountant can accept such quantified information as relevant, verifiable, and free from bias when it comes from qualified practitioners with established professional standards.

Long-lived Intangible Assets

Traditional accounting practice has long followed the rule of recording these assets only to the extent that a verifiable cost has been incurred in their acquisition. (See recommendation VIII, chapter III.) In many cases there is an understatement of the historical cost of these assets. But the difficulties encountered in determining historical cost seem minor when compared with the near-insoluble task of determining the current cost of such assets. Yet some general guidance can be provided as outlined below.

Patents, Trademarks, and Copyrights

In each instance, the uniqueness of the asset involved precludes using the acquisition cost of a similar asset as an approximation of the current cost of the asset under consideration. Questions concerning the accuracy of the historical cost measurement and which index number to use render suspect any measure of current cost derived from an index number adjustment of historical cost. The only feasible alternative embraces the sacrifice of a considerable degree of relevance in order to secure the degree of verifiability and freedom from bias which can be found in adjusting historical cost for general price-level change. Only rarely, and then only momentarily, will there be a verifiable, unbiased approximation of the current cost of an asset of this type as might be found in a valid purchase offer.

Franchises

Occasionally it may be possible to ascertain the current cost of a franchise. This would be true when the grantor of such franchises offers to sell them on a continuing basis. In other cases, general price-level adjustment of historical cost is the only feasible alternative.

Goodwill

The most reasonable approach to the measurement of goodwill in current terms is through the valuation of the entire accounting entity. This procedure involves the estimation of the income to be generated through future operations. As a result, any measurement of goodwill obtained in this manner is lacking in verifiability and is not free from possible bias. Where goodwill has been recorded as a result of a purchase, the unamortized amount may appropriately be adjusted by use of a general price-level index. It does not appear feasible to attempt more than this to obtain a current valuation of goodwill.

A Caveat Repeated

In general, the replacement cost of an asset is considered relevant information. Whether secured by reference to established market price or through application of a price index to acquisition cost, it is sufficiently verifiable and free from bias to gain admission into the accounting information system. It does not automatically follow that current cost should always be the basis for asset valuation. An upper limit exists; an asset should not be reported at its replacement cost if this amount is not recoverable from the revenues generated through its operation or use.

A SET OF ILLUSTRATIVE STATEMENTS

A set of general purpose financial statements is presented in this appendix for the hypothetical XYZ Company, which is assumed to be a corporation organized for profit. The statements are in articulated, comparative form and illustrate a possible approach toward implementing the committee's recommendation for reporting multiple measurements to increase the utility of the information communicated. The statements presented are illustrative of those which a corporation whose securities are generally available to the public might prepare to meet the needs of prospective and present stockholders, creditors, employees, and other interested parties.

Two features distinguish the attached statements from those which might be presented for an actual company. First, the amounts in the attached statements are not rounded (except in one minor instance) so that the approach taken is clearly depicted. Some rounding might well be undertaken in published financial statements. Secondly, rather elaborate and lengthy footnotes, explanations, and schedules accompany the statements presented. These are presented as aids to comprehension and not as models of the types of footnotes, explanations, and schedules which might accompany a set of financial statements of an actual company as supplemental information. Indeed, it is quite probable that, in an introductory period, reasonably detailed and complete footnotes would have to accompany a given corporation's financial statements in order to insure that the information communicated was understood by the largely lay audience to which it is directed.

The model statements attached are designed primarily to illustrate reporting technique and are therefore devoid of argumentation or attempted justification of the types of measurements communicated. As noted previously, their primary purpose is to illustrate a possible approach to the reporting of multiple measurements. Because we have proposed techniques for statement preparation which go beyond conventional practice, numerous footnotes are supplied by way of explanation. Most footnotes are keyed to specific statement items; a few are not.

XYZ COMPANY
Balance Sheet
December 31, 1965

ASSETS

	Historical Cost		Current Cost	
Current Assets				
Cash and Receivables		$ 200,000		$ 200,000
Marketable Securities		50,000		52,000
Inventories:				
Raw Materials	$ 260,000		$ 280,000	
Work in Process	180,000		190,000	
Finished Goods	300,000	740,000	330,000	800,000
Unexpired Insurance and Supplies		10,000		10,000
Total Current Assets		$1,000,000		$ 1,062,000
Investment in Stock of Affiliated Co.		$1,000,000		$ 1,400,000
Property, Plant, and Equipment				
Land		$ 200,000		$ 1,000,000
Buildings and Equipment	$7,000,000		$11,200,000	
Allowance for Depreciation...	3,500,000	3,500,000	5,600,000	5,600,000
Leasehold Interests		1,000,000		1,000,000
Total Property, etc.		$4,700,000		$ 7,600,000
Intangibles				
Patents, Copyrights, etc.		700,000		$ 1,000,000
Total Assets		$7,400,000		$11,062,000

EQUITIES

	Historical Cost		Current Cost	
Current Liabilities				
Lease Obligations (Note A)...	$ 80,000		$ 80,000	
Others unspecified	300,000	$ 380,000	300,000	$ 380,000
Long-Term Liabilities				
Bonds Payable, 5%, Due 19XX	$2,000,000		$ 1,900,000	
Lease Obligations (Note A)...	920,000		920,000	
Deferred Federal Income Taxes Payable	100,000		100,000	
Estimated Taxes on Increases to Current Cost (Note B).....	-0-	3,020,000	1,580,500	4,500,500
Total Liabilities		$3,400,000		$ 4,880,500
Stockholders' Equity				
Capital Stock—$10 par	$3,000,000			
Additional Paid-in Capital....	600,000			
Retained Earnings	400,000			
Total Stockholders' Equity (Note C)		4,000,000		6,181,500
Total Equities		$7,400,000		$11,062,000

Balance-Sheet Notes

Note A—Lease rental payments are $140,000 per annum. Thus at an approximate 6% interest rate, principal is reduced $80,000 the first year. About $55,000 of the second year's payments apply to interest. Accordingly, on the 1965 balance sheet $80,000 of the lease obligation is classed as current and on the 1966 balance sheet $85,000 is similarly classified.

Note B—Stockholders' equity, when assets and liabilities are expressed in current terms, is $3,762,000 larger than when expressed in terms of historical cost before giving consideration to possible Federal income taxes. Since this difference will all be taxed, when and if realized for tax purposes, the entire amount will not accrue to the corporation. The possible applicable taxes were estimated by applying an assumed rate of 50 percent to all differences except that the capital gains rate of 25 percent was applied to the changes in the valuation of marketable securities, investment in stock of affiliated company, and land. Under this approach, the estimated taxes are $1,580,500. The balance of $2,181,500 is carried to stockholders' equity. Estimated taxes on increases to current cost have been included with liabilities in accordance with the discussion in recommendation VI of Chapter III.

Note C—Stockholders' equity in the current-cost columns is presented as a single amount because there is no direct way of ascertaining the current cost of the various elements of paid-in capital except by adjusting contributed capital by a ratio of indices of general purchasing power. But even this becomes unduly complex in circumstances involving a number of stock issuances and the capitalization of retained earnings in distributions of additional shares of stock to stockholders (so-called stock dividends). Presumably legal requirements relative to the segregation and reporting of legal capital and retained earnings can be met through the information presented in the historical-cost columns. Thus, little utility attaches to expressing the traditionally classified elements of stockholders' equity in current terms.

XYZ COMPANY
Balance Sheet
December 31, 1966

ASSETS

	Historical Cost		Current Cost	
Current Assets				
Cash and Receivables		$ 300,000		$ 300,000
Inventories:				
Raw Materials	$ 280,000		$ 300,000	
Work in Process...........	200,000		215,000	
Finished Goods	310,000	790,000	325,000	840,000
Unexpired Insurance and Supplies		20,000		20,000
Total Current Assets........		$1,110,000		$ 1,160,000
Investment in Stock of Affiliated Co.		$1,000,000		$ 1,600,000
Property, Plant, and Equipment				
Land		$ 190,000		$ 1,100,000
Buildings and Equipment......	$8,000,000		$12,900,000	
Allowance for Depreciation....	3,900,000	4,100,000	6,595,000	6,305,000
Leasehold Interests		900,000		945,000
Total Property, etc.........		$5,190,000		$ 8,350,000
Intangibles				
Patents, Copyrights, etc.		$ 600,000		$ 900,000
Total Assets		$7,900,000		$12,010,000

EQUITIES

	Historical Cost		Current Cost	
Current Liabilities				
Lease Obligations (Note A)....	$ 85,000		$ 85,000	
Others unspecified	530,000	$ 615,000	530,000	$ 615,000
Long-Term Liabilities				
Bonds Payable, 5%, Due 19XX	$2,000,000		$ 1,904,500	
Lease Obligations (Note A)....	835,000		835,000	
Deferred Federal Income Taxes Payable	120,000		120,000	
Estimated Taxes on Increases to Current Cost (Note 15).....	—0—	2,955,000	1,725,250	4,584,750
Total Liabilities		$3,570,000		$ 5,199,750
Stockholders' Equity				
Capital Stock—$10 par.......	$3,000,000			
Additional Paid-in Capital.....	600,000			
Retained Earnings	730,000			
Total Stockholders' Equity (Note C)		4,330,000		6,810,250
Total Equities		$7,900,000		$12,010,000

XYZ COMPANY
Income Statement
Year Ended December 31, 1966

	Historical Cost		Current Cost	
Sales (Net)		$20,000,000		$20,000,000
Cost of Goods Sold				
Inventories, Dec. 31, 1965				
(Note 1) .... $	740,000		$ 832,000	
Material, Labor, and Other				
Variable Costs	7,910,000		7,910,400	
Fixed Costs (excl. deprec. &				
amort.)	3,000,000		3,000,000	
Depreciation—Bldg. & Equip.				
(Note 3)	300,000		475,000	
Amortization—Leases				
(Note 5)	100,000		104,000	
Amortization—Patents				
(Note 6)	100,000		160,000	
Current Cost Adjustment				
(Note 10)	—0—		200,000	
	$12,150,000		$12,681,400	
Inventories, Dec. 31, 1966....	790,000	11,360,000	840,000	11,841,400
Gross Margin		$ 8,640,000		$ 8,158,600
Operating Expenses (detail omitted)				
Selling—Variable .... $	2,000,000		$ 2,000,000	
Selling—Fixed (including				
Depreciation—Note 3)	2,000,000		2,042,000	
	$ 4,000,000		$ 4,042,000	
Administrative—Variable ..... $	500,000		$ 500,000	
Administrative—Fixed (including				
Depreciation—Note 3)	3,000,000		3,028,000	
	$ 3,500,000	7,500,000	$ 3,528,000	7,570,000
Net Operating Income..........		$ 1,140,000		$ 588,600
Other Revenue				
Dividends .... $	20,000		$ 20,000	
Gain (Loss) on Sale of				
Marketable Securities (Note 8).	2,000		(2,080)	
Gain on Sale of Land (Note 7).	38,000	60,000	6,400	24,320
		$ 1,200,000		$ 612,920
Other Expenses				
Interest—Bonds (Note 11)..... $	100,000		$ 104,500	
Interest—Leases	60,000	160,000	60,000	164,500
Net Income Before Federal In-				
come Taxes—On Transaction				
Basis		$ 1,040,000		$ 448,420
Federal Income Taxes applicable				
(Note 13)		510,000		256,450
Net Income after Federal Income				
Taxes on Transaction Basis				
(Note 17)		$ 530,000		$ 191,970
Net Gains from Current Cost				
Valuations (Note 16)			$ 600,600	
Federal Income Taxes Applicable				
(Note 13)			398,300	202,300
Purchasing Power Gains on Net				
Debt (Note 12)				187,220
Net Income				$ 581,490

XYZ COMPANY
Statement of Retained Earnings
Year Ended December 31, 1966

	In terms of Historical Cost
Retained Earnings, December 31, 1965	$ 400,000
Net Income	530,000
	$ 930,000
Dividends	200,000
Retained Earnings, December 31, 1966	$ 730,000

XYZ COMPANY
Statement of Stockholders' Equity
Year Ended December 31, 1966

	In terms of Current Cost
Stockholders' Equity, December 31, 1965	$ 6,181,500
Add: Adjustment to restate beginning stockholders' equity in purchasing power equivalents ($6,181,500 × .04)	247,260
Net income for year	581,490
	$ 7,010,250
Less: Dividends	200,000
Stockholders' Equity, December 31, 1966	$ 6,810,250

Assumptions and Explanations

1. Assumed that index of general prices rose four percent on January 1, 1966. Thus, beginning inventories are increased by four percent (see Note 10).

2. Assumed that buildings and equipment replacement cost increased $700,000 gross on January 1, 1966. Such increase is equal to 10 percent of historical cost of $7,000,000. Assumed $1,000,000 (at cost) addition to factory equipment on January 1, 1966.

3. Depreciation for year:

In terms of historical cost

On $7,000,000 balance at 5% ....$ 350,000
On $1,000,000 addition on January 1 at 5% ...   50,000

Total ....$ 400,000

Allowance for Depreciation 12/31/65........ 3,500,000

Allowance for Depreciation 12/31/66........$ 3,900,000

Depreciation of $350,000 is assumed to be chargeable to manufacturing, selling, and administrative functions in the amounts of $250,000, $60,000, and $40,000 respectively.

In terms of current cost:

Current cost on 12/31/65.....$11,200,000
Increase in current cost on
  1/1/66   700,000

Total $11,900,000

Depreciation at 5% .... $ 595,000
Addition on January 1........ 1,000,000
Depreciation at 5% ....ı   50,000

Current cost—12/31/66 ......$12,900,000

Depreciation for year........ $ 645,000
Allowance for Depreciation
  12/31/65 ....$ 5,600,000
Increase to current cost 1/1/66.   350,000   5,950,000

Allowance for Depreciation
  12/31/66 .... $ 6,595,000

Assumed that new equipment is factory equipment. Functional classification of depreciation in current terms is:

Manufacturing:
$250,000 × 170%
($11,900,000 ÷ $7,000,000
= 170%) ....$ 425,000
On new equipment
($1,000,000 at 5%) ....   50,000 $ 475,000

Selling $60,000 × 170%   102,000
Administrative $40,000 ×170%..   68,000

Total as above .... $ 645,000

4. Current cost of buildings and equipment at 12/31/65 .... $11,200,000
Increase in replacement cost as of 1/1/66   700,000

$11,900,000
Current cost at 12/31/65 adjusted for general price-level change
($11,200,000 × 104%)   11,648,000

Gross specific price-level gaiñ...... $ 252,000
Depreciation allowance on replacement cost at 1/1/66
(1/2 of $11,900,000) ....$ 5,950,000
Depreciation allowance as of 12/31/65 adjusted for general price-level change ($5,600,000 × 104%)..   5,824,000   126,000

Net growth in current cost of buildings and equipment .... $ 126,000

Gross change in net book value of property in current terms is $700,000—$350,000 (property is one-half depreciated) or .... $ 350,000

(Difference of $224,000 ($350,000 — $126,000) is due to general price-level change.)

5. It is assumed that the leases were negotiated on December 31, 1965 and that the periodic payments aggregating $140,000 annually were capitalized at 6 percent. For simplicity of illustration, interest on the lease obligation for 1966 is assumed to be $60,000. Rents under leases of this type rose approximately 5 percent as of the end of year.

Amortization of leases for the year adjusted for general price-level change is $100,000 × 104% ...$ 104,000

Specific gain on leases is:

Current cost of unamortized portion of lease assuming an increase of 5 percent in rents on similar leased properties ($900,000 × 1.05)..$ 945,000

Historical cost of unamortized lease interests at December 31, 1966 adjusted for general price-level change of 4 percent ($900,000 × 1.04). 936,000

Specific gain on lease ....$ 9,000

6. The current cost of the patents amortized during the year is assumed to be $160,000 including a specific price increase of $4,000 which occurred during the year. Deflating the remaining $156,000 (divide by 104%), patent amortization for the year expressed in terms of current cost at the beginning of the year is $150,000. Specific gain on patents, then, is:

Current cost of patents—12/31/66 (assumed)...$ 900,000

Unamortized patents at 12/31/66 expressed in terms of 12/31/65 current cost adjusted for general price-level change ($1,000,000 — $150,000) × 104% 884,000

Specific gain on unamortized patents ....$ 16,000

Specific gain on amortized patents............. 4,000

Total gain ....$ 20,000

7. Land with a historical cost of $10,000 and a current cost at 12/31/65 of $40,000 was sold late in 1966 for $48,000. The

gain on the sale, adjusted for general price-level change, to be recognized in 1966 is:

Sales proceeds ....$ 48,000
Current cost at 12/31/65 adjusted for
general price-level change ($40,000
× 104%)   41,600
                                          _____

Gain on parcel sold .... $ 6,400
                                                          ========

Gain on land not sold:
Current cost of land held—assumed.. $1,100,000
Current cost at 12/31/65 of land still
on hand at 12/31/66 adjusted for
general price-level change
($1,000,000 — $40,000) × 104%   998,400
                                          _____

Gain on land not sold .... $ 101,600
                                                      ========

8. Marketable securities with a historical cost of $50,000 were sold for $52,000 during the year. The loss on sale, in current terms, is computed as:

Proceeds ....$ 52,000
Current cost at 12/31/65 adjusted for general price-
level change ($52,000 × 104%)............   54,080
                                             _____
Loss ....$ 2,080
                                              ========

9. The specific gain on investment in stock of affiliated company is:

Current cost at 12/31/66 ....$1,600,000
Current cost at 12/31/65 adjusted for general price-
level change ($1,400,000 × 104%) 1,456,000

Gain on investment in affiliated company ....$ 144,000
                                                 ========

10. The price of materials and other variable costs rose steadily through the year in addition to responding to the general price-level change on January 1. The current cost adjustment of $200,000 consists of the excess of current cost over historical cost for items acquired and used during the year, the excess of current cost at time of use of beginning inventories over their current cost at the beginning of the year, and the excess of current cost of ending inventories over their historical cost. The $400 adjustment for general price-level change on Unexpired Insurance and Supplies is added to Materials, Labor, and other Variable Costs.

11. The $2,000,000 of bonds payable are assumed to call for annual interest payment on December 31. The bonds were valued to yield 5½ percent on December 31, 1965 at which time they had a remaining life of 15 years. The resulting valuation of $1,899,624.19 was rounded to $1,900,000 for illustrative purposes. It is assumed that interest rates did not change during the year. The interest charges for the year and the change in bond valuation, then are:

Interest charges ($1,900,000 × 5½%＝$104,500)	$ 104,500
Interest charges in historical terms (bonds issued at face value) ($2,000,000 × 5%)	100,000
Discount accumulation	$ 4,500
Valuation—December 31, 1965	1,900,000
Valuation—December 31, 1966	$1,904,500

12. The purchasing power gain on net money debt for the year is computed as follows:

Money items	In 1965 $	Equivalent in 1966 $	Gain (loss) in 1966 $
Cash and receivables	$ 200,000	$ 208,000	$ (8,000)
Current liabilities	380,000	395,200	15,200
Deferred Federal income taxes payable	100,000	104,000	4,000
Bonds payable	1,900,000	1,976,000	76,000
Lease obligations	920,000	956,800	36,800
Estimated taxes on increase to current cost	1,580,500	1,643,720	63,220
Total purchasing power gain			$187,220

13. Federal income taxes for 1966 in historical-cost terms are computed as:

Reported net income		$1,040,000
Less capital gains:		
Marketable securities	$ 2,000	
Land	38,000	40,000
Income subject to taxation as ordinary income		$1,000,000
Tax at assumed rate of 50 percent		$ 500,000
Capital gains taxes ($40,000 × 25 percent)		10,000
Total Federal income taxes for 1966.		$ 510,000

The above computation ignores the dividend exclusion provision of current tax law and also assumes that the treatment accorded leases is acceptable for tax purposes. It is further assumed that an additional $40,000 of depreciation was taken for tax purposes which, under tax allocation procedures, requires a credit to the deferred taxes payable account of $20,000 (50 percent tax rate assumed).

Federal income taxes in current terms are computed as follows:

	Transaction-based Income	Net Gains from Current-Cost Valuations	Total
Net income before taxes as reported in income statement	$448,420	$600,600	$1,049,020
Add: Adjustments to restate historical costs in purchasing power equivalents which are taxed as if income:			
Inventory ($800,000 x .04)	32,000		32,000
Buildings and equipment*	22,400	201,600	224,000
Leases (note 5)	4,000	36,000	40,000
Patents (note 6)	6,000	34,000	40,000
Land (note 7)	1,600	38,400	40,000
Marketable securities (note 8)	2,080**	—0—	2,080
Unexpired Ins. & Sup. (note 10)	400	—0—	400
Investment in affiliated company (note 9)	—0—	56,000	56,000
Amounts subject to present or future taxation	$516,900	$966,600	$1,483,500
Less items subject to taxation as capital gains:			
Investment in affiliated company	$—0—	$200,000	$ 200,000
Land	8,000	140,000	148,000
Total	$ 8,000	$340,000	$ 348,000
Balance subject to taxation as ordinary income	$508,900	$626,600	$1,135,500
Income taxes at assumed rate of 50 percent	$254,450	$313,300	$ 567,750
Capital gains tax at 25 percent on above items	2,000	85,000	87,000
Total Federal taxes applicable	$256,450***	$398,300	$ 654,750

*Current cost of equipment and buildings at January 1, 1966 is $11,200,000 with accumulated depreciation equal to $5,600,000. Adjustment for 4 percent general price-level change then is ($11,200,000 — $5,600,000) × .04, or $224,000. Adjustment applicable to depreciation charged to operations in 1966 is $11,200,000 × .05 × .04 (cost times depreciation rate times general price-level increase) or $22,400.

**In current terms, a loss of $2,080 was recognized upon the sale of the marketable securities. This loss exactly equals the adjustment for general price-level change, see note 8. The sale of the securities should have no effect upon the taxes assigned to 1966 since the securities were sold at their current cost as of the beginning of the year and current tax law does not recognize changes in the purchasing power of the dollar in the determination of taxable income. Adding back the $2,080 exactly cancels the loss recognized.

***Federal income taxes may appear to be disproportionately large relative to income. This is due to the fact that these taxes are levied upon capital when money income is taxed without giving effect to the purchasing-power equivalents of the dollar measurements involved.

14. The balance in the Estimated Taxes on Increases to Current Cost account is computed as follows:

Excess of current cost over historical cost:

Inventories	$ 50,000	
Leases	45,000	
Buildings and equipment	2,205,000	
Patents	300,000	
Excess of face value over current value of bonds payable	95,500	
Total	$2,695,500	
Tax at assumed 50 percent rate		$1,347,750
Investment in affiliated company	$ 600,000	
Land	910,000	
Total	$1,510,000	
Tax at 25 percent capital gains rate		377,500
Gross increase in stockholders' equity	$4,205,500	
Estimated taxes on increases to current cost		$1,725,250

15. Reconciliation of balance in Estimated Taxes on Increases to Current Cost as between December 31, 1965 and December 31, 1966:

Balance, December 31, 1965 ...... $1,580,500

Federal income taxes accrued on income in current-cost terms for 1966:

On transaction basis............$ 256,450

On net gains from current-cost valuations   398,300

Total ....$ 654,750

Federal income taxes in historical-cost terms   510,000   144,750

Balance, December 31, 1966 ...... $1,725,250

16. Gains from changes in current-cost valuations recognized during 1966 are:

Inventories (note 10) ....$ 200,000

Investment in affiliated company (note 9)   144,000

Land (note 7)   101,600

Buildings and equipment (note 4)...   126,000

Leases (note 5)   9,000

Patents (note 6)   20,000

Net gains ....$ 600,600

17. Net income for 1966 in terms of historical cost adjusted for changes in the purchasing power of the dollar is presented below and is based upon the following assumptions: (1) general price level has risen 40 percent (including 4 percent rise on January 1, 1966) since land, buildings, and equipment were acquired; (2) general price level has risen 20 percent, including January 1, 1966, rise, since patents were acquired; (3) general price level has risen only

the January 1, 1966, rise of 4 percent since marketable securities were acquired.

Reported net income in historical terms.........$ 530,000

Add: Gain on net money debt (as in note 12 excluding $63,220 and except that gain on bonds payable would be $2,000,000 × 1.04—$2,000,000, or $80,000)......... 128,000

$ 658,000

Less: Additions to cost caused by restating historical cost in terms of purchasing power equivalents:

Depreciation adjustment
($350,000 × .40).........$140,000

Inventory adjustment
($740,000 × .04) 29,600

Unexpired Insurance and Supplies adjustment ($10,000 × .04). 400

Lease amortization adjustment
($100,000 × .04) 4,000

Patent amortization adjustment
($100,000 × .20) 20,000

Cost of land sold adjustment
($10,000 × .40).......... 4,000

Cost of marketable securities sold adjustment ($50,000 × .04). 2,000 $ 200,000

Net income in terms of constant units (December 31, 1966 dollars) of purchasing power ....$ 458,000

COMMITTEE ASSENT AND A COMMENTARY

When the Committee to Prepare a Statement of Basic Accounting Theory was appointed, it was assured that its final statement would be published provided at least two-thirds of the members assented. All nine committee members assented to publication; however, in doing so one member submitted the following comments with the request that they be included in the publication.

Committee to Prepare a Statement of
Basic Accounting Theory

NORTON M. BEDFORD
R. LEE BRUMMET
NEIL C. CHURCHILL
PAUL E. FERTIG
RUSSELL H. MORRISON
ROLAND F. SALMONSON
GEORGE H. SORTER
LAWRENCE L. VANCE
CHARLES T. ZLATKOVICH,
Chairman

COMMENTS OF RUSSELL H. MORRISON

This is a thoughtful and, I believe, useful study of certain aspects of the field of accounting—mainly the standards for identifying, measuring and communicating accounting information, the needs of the users of such information, and some thoughts on the nature and scope of accounting in the future. But it offers little in the way of basic accounting theory as a foundation for a body of sound accounting principles governing the treatment of accounting information. Thus, in this respect I believe that an essential part of the statement of basic accounting theory which the committee was charged to prepare remains to be developed. My further comments are limited to three principal matters.

In Chapter III, the study advocates reporting on the basis of current-cost information to supplement the historical-cost statements. I do not disagree that it would be useful if such current-cost information could be developed on a sound and practicable basis. But with all due respect to the presentation made in Appendices A and B, in my judgment there have yet to be devised feasible and acceptable methods for objectively determining current cost, except perhaps in such areas as marketable securities. Since I do not concur in the recommendation for presenting current-cost information, I offer no specific comments on the method and presentation proposed in these appendices.

Instead of current-cost information, it would, in my opinion, be useful and practicable to supplement the historical-cost reports with statements or summarized information adjusted for the effect of general price-level changes, i.e., changes in the purchasing power of the dollar.* And where inflation is significant, this becomes necessary if the misleading inferences of historical-cost reports are to be avoided.

Chapter IV is a useful discussion of accounting information for internal management. But I do not see that it has a place in this study, at least to the extent it is developed here. The information system in any enterprise must be a unified whole. It produces a flow of data from the point of origin to the external users. As this information flows through the system, it is used at many points and in many forms by various levels of management for planning, control and decision-making. The basic accounting theory, concepts or standards which govern the flow of data into and through the information system are the same irrespective of the stage at which the information is extracted and used.

Chapter V is an interesting look into the nature and scope of accounting in the future as it may be affected by advances in methods of gathering, processing, storing, communicating and presenting accounting information. While all of this may make possible great improvements in the planning, control and decision-making, I do not see that it has anything to do with a statement of basic accounting theory.

---

*AICPA Accounting Research Study No. 6, **Reporting the Financial Effects of Price-Level Changes**, 1963.

INDEX

A

Accounting,
   concepts, 69
   defined, 1
   method of, 6
   scope of, 5
Accounting information
   (see also "Users' needs")
   appropriateness to expected use,
   14-15
   communication of, 13-14, 64
   consistency of practices, 18
   disclosure of significant
   relationships, 15-16
   environmental, 16-17
   standards for, 2
   uniformity, 17-18
Accounting model (system), 37-39,
   41, 50, 56-59, 61, 64, 67-68, 71
Activities,
   programmed, 43-44, 45, 47, 49
   unprogrammed, 43-44, 46, 49
Alternatives (see also "Control" and
   "Planning"), 45-47, 50, 60
American Accounting Association,
   30, 37
American Institute of CPAs, 30

B

Behavior, 20, 63, 64, 68, 69-70
Bias (see also "Freedom from bias"),
   11, 17, 29, 54, 74, 76
Budgets, 5, 41, 49, 54, 58, 61

C

Cash Flow Projections, 23, 24, 25, 34,
   38, 60, 61
Committee assent and commentary,
   97-98
Communication of accounting
   information, 13-14, 64
Computers, 17, 59, 60, 61, 63, 64,
   66, 68, 69
Consistency, 18, 55

Contracts, executory, 32-33
Control, 37, 43, 45-46, 48-50, 54, 58,
   61-62, 68
Conversions, 35-36
Current-cost data, means of obtaining,
   73-79
Current-cost information, 19, 28-32,
   34, 65, 79

D

Decision making, 4, 14-15, 20, 38,
   40, 42, 44, 47, 51, 61, 66, 68
Decision models, 19, 22, 26-27, 36, 48,
   60, 70
Deferred taxes, 34-35
Depreciation, 29, 35
Discovery values, 34, 78

E

Earnings, prediction of, 23-25, 34, 61
Economic information, 1, 2, 6, 41,
   57, 59
Environmental information, 16, 25,
   34, 55
Executory contracts, 32-33

F

Financial Executives Institute, 30
Financial position, 24-25, 58
Fixed assets, 75-78
Freedom from bias, 7, 11, 28-29, 31,
   32, 53-54

G

Generally accepted principles, 6, 16
Goals (see "Planning")
Guidelines for accounting information,
   13-18, 55-56
Guidelines,
   appropriateness to expected use,
   14-15

99